SPEAKING PICTURES

A Gallery of Pictorial Poetry
from the Sixteenth Century
to the Present

SPEAKING PICTURES

A Gallery of Pictorial Poetry
from the Sixteenth Century
to the Present

EDITED BY MILTON KLONSKY

HARMONY BOOKS
a division of Crown Publishers, Inc.
New York

Harmony Books, a division of Crown Publishers, Inc.
419 Park Avenue South
New York, New York 10016

Copyright © 1975 by Milton Klonsky
Printed in the United States of America
Published simultaneously in Canada by General
Publishing Company Limited

Library of Congress Catalog Card Number: 75-29920

Publisher: BRUCE HARRIS
Editor: LINDA SUNSHINE
Assoc. Editor: NANCY CROW
Production: GENE CONNER, MURRAY SCHWARTZ

Library of Congress Cataloging in Publication Data
Main entry under title:

Speaking pictures.

  Bibliography: p.
  Includes index.
  1. Poetry, Modern. 2. Emblems. 3. Concrete poetry.
I. Klonsky, Milton.
PN6101.S6   808.81   75-29920
ISBN 0-517-52376-0
ISBN 0-517-52377-9 pbk.

Acknowledgments and Copyright Notices

808.81
S741
1975

in Concrete, Indiana University Press. Copyright, ©, 1966, by Mary Ellen Solt. Reprinted by permission of the author.

SOMETHING ELSE PRESS, INC. for "Glass" by Dick Higgins, copyright, ©, 1971, by Something Else Press, Inc., reprinted by permission of Dick Higgins and Something Else Press, Inc.; for "Wind" by Eugen Gomringer from *The Book of Hours and Constellations,* copyright, ©, 1968, by Something Else Press, Inc., reprinted by permission of Eugen Gomringer and Something Else Press, Inc.

JORDAN STECKEL for "Logopolis." Copyright, ©, 1971, by Jordan Steckel. Reprinted by permission of the author.

SALETTE TAVARES for "Aranha." Reprinted by permission of the author.

UNIVERSITY OF CALIFORNIA PRESS for "Flowerishes" from *Collected Poems* by Kenneth Burke, published in 1968. Originally published by the University of California Press. Reprinted by permission of The Regents of the University of California.

THE UNIVERSITY OF CHICAGO PRESS for "Wei Chuang" by James Liu from *The Art of Chinese Poetry* (University of Chicago Press, 1962). Reprinted by permission of the publisher.

THE VIKING PRESS, INC. for excerpt from *Finnegans Wake* by James Joyce. Copyright, 1939, by James Joyce; copyright renewed, ©, 1967, by George Joyce and Lucia Joyce. Reprinted by permission of The Viking Press, Inc., and Society of Authors.

WALTER VERLAG AG OLTEN for woodcut from *Alchemy: Science of the Cosmos, Science of the Soul* by Titus Burckhardt. Copyright, ©, 1960, by Walter Verlag Ag Olten. Reprinted by permission of the publisher.

EMMETT WILLIAMS for "Like Attracts Like" and "She Loves Me" from *An Anthology of Concrete Poetry* edited by Emmett Williams, copyright, ©, 1971, and *Material,* copyright, ©, 1958. Reprinted by permission of the author and Something Else Press, Inc.

JONATHAN WILLIAMS for "Five Jargonelles from the Herbalist's Notebook" from *Blues and Roots/Rue and Bluets* by Jonathan Williams, copyright, ©, 1971, by Grossman Publishers. Reprinted by permission of the author and Grossman Publishers.

PEDRO XISTO for "Epithalamium—II" and "Wind-Leaf." Reprinted by permission of the author.

Contents

Introduction

Painting is mute poetry, poetry a speaking picture.
     —Simonides of Ceos, sixth century B.C.

    Property was thus appall'd
    That the self was not the same;
    Single nature's double name
    Neither two nor one was called.
        —Wm. Shakespeare, *The Phoenix and The Turtle*

SPEAKING PICTURES: *A Gallery of Pictorial Poetry* brings together for the first time many of the chief works in a five-hundred-year-old yet still obscure tradition that, from the start, has been cast inevitably under the spell of Hermes. Throughout one can trace the presence of this elusive twilight god, famous for his benevolent duplicity, who loved to pose riddles and play practical jokes. For, as we have come to recognize—but only after one of the most baffling double-takes in literature—the genre of the picture-poem and/or poem-picture, with its reciprocal *presto-chango* of form, originated in Italy during the early Renaissance mainly as the result of what later proved to be a misconception of Egyptian hieroglyphs; then spread from Italy to all the centers of European culture, reaching its height in critical esteem and popularity by the mid-seventeenth century; after which, following a long period of decline, when picture-poetry as such seemed almost forgotten, it has only recently reemerged in our own time as the result of a strangely similar misconception of Chinese ideograms. How all this came about is perhaps better shown than told, for Hermes's sleight-of-hand still has to be seen to be believed.

Around the year 1460, as it happened, within a decade of the fall of Contantinople to the Turks, there was smuggled out of Byzantium to the circle of humanist scholars at the court of the Medici in Florence a collection of rare and ancient Greek manuscripts. Among them were certain mystical dialogues, called the

Corpus Hermeticum, in which an Egyptian hierophant (high priest) cast in the role of Hermes Trismegistus ("Thrice-Great Hermes") reveals the sacred mysteries to his disciple Asclepius. Historians nowadays have determined that these works, combining neoplatonist metaphysics, Persian mithraism, gnostic theosophy, magical incantations, and alchemical prescriptions, were composed in Alexandria sometime between 100-300 A.D., and probably served as the bible of an Egyptian religious cult; but at the time of their rediscovery in Florence they were hailed as a godsend out of remote antiquity, before the days of Moses, and to have been written by Hermes Trismegistus himself. "This huge historical error," asserts the Renaissance scholar Frances A. Yates, in her *Giordano Bruno and the Hermetic Tradition,* "was to have amazing results."

The legendary Hermes Trismegistus (or "Mercurius," as he is also called) had been described by Cicero in his *De Natura Deorum* as the culture hero who, during a sojourn in Egypt, assumed the identity of the god Thoth, inventor of hieroglyphs, and founded the holy city of Hermopolis. Following Cicero, St. Augustine as well as the Church Fathers Clement of Alexandria and Lactantius repeated this legend of Hermes Trismegistus, whom they regarded as the author of the so-called "hermetic" doctrines on black magic and idolatry that had sprung up about his name. So then, in turn, with the real existence of Hermes Trismegistus thus affirmed on such high authority, both pagan and Christian, the neoplatonist philosopher-poet Marsilio Ficino, who first translated the *Corpus Hermeticum,* assumed without question that Hermes Trismegistus had actually lived and taught in Egypt at one time. "In that age in which Moses was born," wrote Ficino, accepting the weird geneology devised by St. Augustine, "flourished Atlas the astrologer, brother of Prometheus the physicist and maternal uncle of the elder Mercury, whose nephew was Mercurius Trismegistus." But then Ficino made a claim of his own just as astonishing: the Egyptian magus was declared to have been the pristine source of a sacred wisdom, a *prisca theologia,* no less, that had been passed on down the ages and through the sages in an unbroken succession from Orpheus to Pythagoras to Plato to Plotinus . . . up to, presumably, Ficino himself. For it was Ficino, along with his cospirit and disciple Pico della Mirandola, who became the apostles of that mystical Renaissance neoplatonism, with its newly discovered "hermetic" core of magic, which complemented but also in some ways rivaled the account of creation told in *Genesis*.

As envisioned in this cosmogony, the Mind of God, which contains all possible ideas as *logoi spermatikoi,* penetrates and impregnates the World Soul brooding over nature, thereby generating the forms infused into matter that are perceived by the senses. "Every particular thing," wrote Plotinus in the *Enneads,* "is the image within matter of the Intellectual Principle, which itself images the Divine Being; thus, each entity in the natural world is linked to that Divine Being in whose likeness it is made." The universe was conceived as a vast rebus, a cosmic riddle whose spiritual meaning lay hidden under the appearances of nature. In "imitating" nature, therefore, Renaissance artists under the spell of the hermetic philosophy mimicked the primal act of God himself, and their own creations stood to the larger Creation as microcosm to macrocosm. Such multilayered pictures as Botticelli's *Birth of Venus,* say, or Titian's *Sacred and Profane Love,* or Leonardo's *Leda and the Swan* were meant to be "read" hermeneutically for their symbolical and allegorical content—"seen," that is, with the mind's eye—for their poetic ideas to be made visible and their images to speak for themselves.

But all this is only part of the picture and/or story. For about the year 1419, long before the *Corpus Hermeticum* was discovered, there had arrived in Italy another apparent godsend of a manuscript out of Byzantium, the so-called *Hieroglyphika* of Horapollo (Horus Apollo). And here again this treatise, which claimed to have deciphered the *hieroglyphika grammata* ("sacred carved letters") of ancient Egypt, was also mistakenly believed to have been written in remote antiquity. As the *Corpus Hermeticum* had seemed to Ficino and his circle to contain a pure gnosis, unmediated by discursive reasoning, so also the *Hieroglyphika* might unriddle for them the secrets of a written language that reflected ideas directly, what (so to speak) the Sphinx would have spoken if it spoke in images rather than words. Horapollo, an Egyptian-born scribe who lived in Constantinople sometime in the fifth century A.D., assumed that hieroglyphs were simple pictographs—as in fact they had been around 3000 B.C. during the earliest stage of their evolution—so that his interpretations, though occasionally close to the mark, were no more than wild, if wildly ingenious, guesses. It was not of course until Champollion, as late as 1824, finally deciphered

Manuscript of the Middle Kingdom (c. 1785 B.C.)

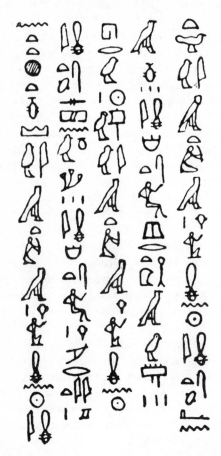

TRANSLITERATION	ENGLISH TRANSLATION

·t. *iw mt m-ḥr·i min, my šty 'n-*
tyw, my ḥmšt ḥr ḥt'w
hrw t'w. iw mt m-ḥr·i myn
my šty sšnw, my ḥmšt ḥr mryt
nt iḫt . iw mt m-ḥr·i myn my

(Figure 1)

Death is before me to-day
As the odour of myr/rh,
As when one sitteth under the sail/
    On a windy day.

Death is before me to-day/
As the odour of lotus flowers,
As when one sitteth on the shore/
    Of drunkenness.

Death is before me to-day
As . . .

hieroglyphs with the aid of the Rosetta Stone that they were understood to be characters in a primitive syllabary, somewhat like our own alphabet, that signified not ideas as such but vocal sounds forming words. *(Fig. 1)*

Horapollo's *Hieroglyphika,* first published in Latin by the Venetian printer Aldus in 1505, appeared at a time when the invention of printing and the spread of literacy throughout Europe was in the process of transforming what had once been predominantly an aural into a visual culture. The book was subsequently translated into most European languages and published in numerous editions before the end of the century. Even the skeptical Erasmus, while dismissing as folly and superstition the notion that hieroglyphs were a "sacred language," believed they might serve as the model for a universal symbology of ideas that could be "seen through" as well as read—"a pure transparency," as Coleridge once expressed it, "that intercepts no light and adds no stain"—and thus constitute a sort of philosophical algebra for the family of mankind. The great French printer and neoplatonist mystic Geofroy Tory, whose *Champ Fleury* in 1529 was inspired by the *Hieroglyphika,* attempted to devise such an international iconic alphabet by recasting the shapes and proportions of letters. And his own typographical designs, though they never fulfilled the high purpose for which they were invented, led to other experiments by the master printers of the Renaissance. *(Fig. 2-3)*

For most artists and poets of that era, who regarded as self-evident Horace's gnomic remark, *Ut pictura poesis* ("As is poetry so is painting"), this very resemblance, so close that they seemed integral, also suggested that a disintegration must have occurred in the past. The belief was then widely held that in some lost arcadian foretime mankind had actually possessed a single sacred language in which idea and image were one. Thus, on the margin of a copy of the *Hieroglyphika,* Albrecht Dürer drew a number of sketches illustrating Horapollo's essentially poetic interpretations, which, had he done so for the rest, would have made it the earliest book of what came to be known as "Emblem poetry." *(Fig. 4)*

That, it turned out, was to be Andrea Alciati's *Emblematum Liber,* published in 1531, not only the most famous but the prototype of all that followed. The engravings by various artists and the accompanying poems by Alciati, mainly translations from the *Greek Anthology,* were conceived as indivisible, meant to reflect,

UTOPIAN AND VOLUNTARY LETTERS

"I have added also the *Utopian* letters . . . which we might call *Voluntary* letters, made at one's pleasure, as are those which the makers of ciphers . . . drew in such shape and form as they chose" (Geofroy Tory). *(Figure 2)*

FANTASTIC LETTERS

"Concerning our *Fantastic* letters, I say that in imitation of the Egyptian manner of writing, they are made by symbols and pictures, but not in accordance with natural philosophy, like those of the Egyptians. The first is an A, represented by an open compass; the second is a B, represented by a *fusy* [the steel used for striking fire from a flint]; the third is a C, represented by a handle; and so on" (Geofroy Tory).   *(Figure 3)*

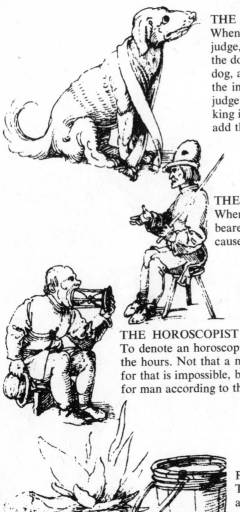

THE JUDGE
When they denote a magistrate or judge, they place the royal stole beside the dog, who is naked. Since just as the dog, as said above, gazes intently upon the images of the gods, so the archon-judge of ancient times contemplated the king in his nakedness. Whereupon they add the royal stole to this figure.

THE SHRINE-BEARER
When they wish to indicate a shrine-bearer, they draw a house-guard, because by him is the temple guarded.

THE HOROSCOPIST
To denote an horoscopist, they draw a man eating the hours. Not that a man actually eats the hours, for that is impossible, but because food is prepared for man according to the hour.

PURITY
To depict purity, they draw fire and water. For through these elements are all things purified.

Hieroglyphical sketches drawn by Albrecht Dürer on the back of a Latin translation of Horapollo made by the artist's friend Pirkheimer.   *(Figure 4)*

and to reflect upon, one another in multiple facets of meaning.
Here, for example, is Alciati's *Emblema 132,* with the motto:
"From the pursuit of literature one acquires immortality":

Ex litterarum ſtudijs immortalitatem acquiri.

EMBLEMA 132.

NEPTUNI *tubicen (cuius pars vltima cetum*
Æquoreum facies indicat eſſe Deum)
Serpentis medio Triton comprendi ur orbe,
Qui caudam inſerto mord cùs ore tenet.
Fama viros animo inſignes , præclaraque geſta
Proſequitur ; toto mandat , & orbe legi.

An English version of the poem by George Boas (who was,
incidentally, also the modern editor of the *Hieroglyphika*) reads
as follows:

Neptune's trumpeter, whose body is a sea-beast and whose appearance
shows that he is a sea-god, Triton, is enclosed in a circle made by a
serpent which holds its tail in its mouth [Uroboros, symbol of im-
mortality]. Fame follows men outstanding in mental powers and
glorious deeds, and demands that their name be spread throughout
the world.

Upon which Boas comments: "Literally, the picture is of a sea-
beast blowing a trumpet as he rises from the waves. Allegorically,
the beast is the god Triton, blowing a conch. Tropologically, the

trumpet is fame and the serpent eternity. Anagogically, it conveys the message contained in the motto heading the picture . . ." and so forth.

The intellectual effort required to "get the picture" was intended by Alciati as a necessary veil, or cloud-cover, to conceal the mysteries from the profane. (Hermes, among his other magical functions, was both a gatherer and disperser of mists and clouds.) Even more cryptic emblems called *imprese*—whose meanings, for most people at that time, as for us, lay buried within their crypts— became fashionable throughout Europe in the following decades, pointing the way for the inwrought "metaphysical" style in poetry represented by Gongora in Spain, Scève in France, Marino in Italy, Donne in England.

Nature itself, as the Logos of God brought down to earth and made manifest, was not exempt from such riddling obfuscation. One Italian enthusiast, the poet Emanuele Tesauro, visualized the sky in the image of "a vast cerulean shield, or empty canvas, or blank page, on which skillful Nature draws what she meditates: forming heroical devices, and mysterious and witty symbols of her secrets"; and, as such, the thunderbolts of Jove-Jehovah could be no less than cosmic wisecracks, "formidable witticisms of God, having the bolt of lightning for their device and the thunder for their motto." In sum, the Emblem of emblems. Shakespeare might have had this sort of hieroglyphical frenzy in mind when he wrote the passage in *Hamlet* (Act III, Scene 2) wherein the merry Dane taunts Polonius by persuading him to interpret then reinterpret the mercurially shifting rorschach-blot of a cloud:

> *Ham.:* Do you see yonder cloud that's almost in shape of a camel?
> *Pol.:* By the mass, and 'tis like a camel indeed.
> *Ham.:* Methinks it is like a weasel.
> *Pol.:* It is backed like a weasel.
> *Ham.:* Or like a whale?
> *Pol.:* Very like a whale.

The cult of Emblem poetry, and the hermetic philosophy which was its source, had been established in Europe for half a century before reaching Elizabethan England. But by 1583, when the most celebrated Magus of the age, Giordano Bruno (considered by some scholars to have been Shakespeare's model for the exiled wizard Prospero in *The Tempest*) took refuge from the Inquisition in England, where he sojourned for a year at Oxford, he found there many devoted as well as powerful adherents to his cause. Bruno received the patronage of the poet-courtier Sir Philip Sidney, in whose circle at the time was the young Edmund Spenser, who, as his work attests, must also have been initiated into the mysteries. Spenser had already published the emblematic pastorals of *The Shepherd's Calendar,* and was then engaged in weaving the elaborate and inwrought tapestry of that "dark conceit" (as he called it) which became *The Fairie Queene.* By its fusion of medieval allegory and Italian epic romance, classical mythology and Christian theology, in an indivisible compact, *The Fairie Queene* was conceived in the same spirit that had produced Emblem poetry.

In fact, the first such collection in English, Geoffrey Whitney's *Choice of Emblemes,* published in Leyden in 1586, reveals throughout the influence of Spenser's poetic vision and ideas. "Herein," declared Whitney in his Preface, "by the office of the eie, and the eare, the mind may reape dooble delighte through holsome precepts, shadowed with pleasant devises." In keeping with the magpie custom of the time, Whitney had filched the engravings and most of the accompanying poems (which he later translated) for his book from the many collections of Emblem poetry that had appeared on the continent; and, in turn, Elizabethan poets, designers and artists not only reaped "dooble delighte" from his *Choice of Emblemes* but distilled from it imagery to produce their own works. Queen Elizabeth herself, it is said, encouraged the vogue for emblems at the court by having a jacket bejewelled and embroidered with "pleasant devises" copied from Whitney. Emblems and *imprese* of all sorts now figured in heraldry, tournaments, carvings, tapestries, pageants, and, especially, in those communal theatrical extravaganzas of the nobility (once characterized by Ben Jonson as "court hieroglyphs") known as masques.

It was through masques, as Frances A. Yates has pointed out in her *Theatre of the World,* that "the connection in the Renaissance mind between magic and mechanics finds expression . . . and in them mechanics were being used, partially at least, to form a vast moving and changing talisman which should call down divine powers to the assistance of the monarch." Allegorical figures who personified Justice, Truth or Beauty in a masque by Ben Jonson, as produced and staged by Inigo Jones, were actually thought to contain within themselves some trace of the original ideas of Justice, Truth or Beauty within God's Mind. This "natural" magic, as Ficino called it—to distinguish it from the "black" magic of sorcerers in cahoots with Satan—was accomplished by a reverse upward movement along the great spiritual chain of neoplatonism, whereby "every entity is linked to that Divine Being in whose likeness it is made," just as the ancient Egyptian priests described in the *Corpus Hermeticum* once made the statues of the gods in their temples move and speak.

Likewise, the so-called "iconic," or shaped, poems of George Puttenham, George Herbert, Robert Herrick, et al.—among the earliest examples of a genre that appears throughout this *Gallery* —also assumed a magical reciprocity between printed words shaped into images and the ideas they both contained and reflected. The picture-poem so conceived might be considered an amulet, even a sort of primitive fetish. Though the makers of iconic poems could hardly have been aware of this at the time, by such typographical necromantics they were conjuring up the instinctive religious rites of a true pristine theology, or *prisca theologia,* far more ancient than ancient Egypt's, in use before the invention of writing, relics of which can be found in the magic-working pictures of totemic animals painted on walls of caves like those at Lascaux and Altamira millennia ago. A superstitious belief in the substantiality of names and images—and their consubstantiality— underlies all mythical thinking. As Ernst Cassirer points out: "The image or name does not represent the 'thing,' it *is* the thing; it does not merely stand for the object, but has the same actuality." And from this belief stems the principle of *pars pro toto,* the part standing for the whole as species to genus, microcosm to macro-cosm—and thus "linked" as an idea to Ficino's own natural magic —which makes possible the hocus-pocus of spells and charms as well as the presto-chango of metaphor.*

---

* An Egyptian myth tells how the goddess Isis once compelled the sun god Ra by sorcery to reveal his secret name, thereby obtaining dominion over him and all his power. In the name of Ra, incidentally, and its hieroglyph—which survives as our astronomic symbol for the sun—we can also find the Indo-European root of the words *rajah* and *rex,* perhaps pointing to a common derivation. A palimpsest-echo of the great picture-name itself, reaching us from the depths of the Pliocene (anything so far-out has to be far-fetched) may still be heard in one of the earliest cries of proto-human language: the wide-open-mouthed, sun-greeting *rrrrrrrahhhh-rrrrrrrahhhh* growled by lemurs at dawn along the Ganges and the Nile. Cheerleaders nowadays still rouse themselves into eurhythmic frenzies of propitiation with the same primordial *rrrrrrrahhhh.* "One thought," as Blake said, "fills eternity."

Toward the end of Elizabeth's reign in England, the widespread diffusion, and hence vulgarization, of hermeticist literature down to the pious and upward striving middle classes, was regarded by its votaries as something of a sacrilege. But this process, swelled by the social and religious tendencies of the age, was to continue deep into the next century.

"The century which produced the greatest mystics," declares Mario Praz, "produced also the Emblem poets: they seem opposites, yet frequently these opposites are found united in the same person." That baroque passion for the joining of contraries into a higher unity, a *discordia concors,* which was shared by all these visionary poets, would be exemplified accordingly even in their own lives. At the time, however, they were dragooned and impressed into the total religious civil war dividing Europe between the forces of the Protestant Reformation and Catholic Counter-Reformation. Such suspiciously heretical doctrines as the *prisca theologia* of Hermes Trismegistus, "natural" magic, cabalistical abracadabra, and so forth, were now muffled or suppressed on both sides; and Emblem poetry came to assume instead an almost entirely pietistic and evangelical character. The picture-poem itself was no longer conceived in a mystical sense as a higher unity, but rather separated hyphenetically as sermon (poem) to text (picture). Mysticism, as Cardinal Newman once cracked, wisely, "begins in mist and ends in schism."

What still endured, nonetheless, was a neoplatonist faith in the essential oneness of the Word and the Work—both having issued from the Mind of the Creator—so that Nature was often referred to as God's other "Book." The most famous of seventeenth-century English Emblem poets, Francis Quarles, declared: "Before the knowledge of letters, God was known by *Hieroglyphicks;* and, indeed, what are the Heaven, the Earth, nay every creature, but *Hieroglyphicks* and Emblems of His Glory?" And Quarles's contemporary, John Milton, whose *Paradise Lost* was intended to add to that Glory, asked almost the same rhetorical question:

> What if earth
> Be but the shadow of Heaven, and things therein
> Each to each other like, more than on earth is thought?

Quarles qua poet hardly deserves comparison nowadays with Milton, yet during their own lifetimes, as Horace Walpole observed: "Milton had to wait for his due until the world had finished admiring Quarles." His *Emblemes,* published in 1635, was the most widely read book of poetry of any sort in the seventeenth century, suiting the taste of the age for metaphysical fancy and moral self-flagellation. Though he declared himself "a true sonne of the Church of England," Quarles had no scruple in taking his emblems from Jesuit collections published in Europe; nor, for that matter, did his fellow Emblem poets, such as Christopher Harvey or Robert Farley or even the fanatically anti-Catholic George Wither, who used the emblems against themselves as texts on which to preach an opposing faith. Some occasional squibs and flashes of wit in these poems serve now and then to relieve an otherwise impenetrable miasma of Calvinist gloom. Still, their bathetic religiosity has in the course of time acquired a modern patina of "camp," which may yet save them entirely from oblivion.

The great English poet-mystics of the seventeenth century, who include Donne and Herbert, Vaughn and Crashaw, worked outside the tradition of Emblem poetry. Yet they were all nonetheless profoundly influenced in their style and sensibility. Of Crashaw, especially, the assertion has often been made by critics that his rhapsodic hymns lack only the accompanying emblems to have become the masterpieces of that genre. Crashaw's own spiritual agony, in which he was torn (as he wrote) "twixt in and out, twixt life and death," finally to be resolved by his self-exile and conversion to Catholicism in Rome, foreshadowed the conflicting religious and political passions that later erupted into civil war in England.

The midpoint of the century was also the zenith of Emblem poetry. With the Restoration of Charles II in 1660, after the long interregnum of the Puritan Commonwealth, the wits and wordlings of the court must have found Emblem poetry itself emblematic of the religious bigotry and obscurantism of a time best forgotten. But, most important, the neoplatonist cosmology which had provided its *raison d'être* was to be displaced in the following decades by the new scientific world order of Newton and Descartes. The rift between mind and matter, the Word and the Work, henceforth grew steadily wider; and man himself, from being the microcosm of the Creator, became a mere spectator, enclosed within his own sensorium, of a world indifferent to his existence—"a world," as the philosopher E. A. Burtt has put it, "hard, cold, colorless, silent and dead; a world of quantity; a world of mathematically computable motions in mechanical regularity"—which is to say, the sort of world we still make do with.

The last noteworthy collection of English Emblem poetry, John Bunyan's *Divine Emblems; or, Temporal Things Spiritualized,* with the subtitle, *Calculated for the Use of Young People,* appeared in 1686, exactly a hundred years after the publication of Geoffrey Whitney's *Choice of Emblemes.* What Bunyan's own homespun Baptist allegory, *The Pilgrim's Progress,* was to Spenser's *The Fairie Queene,* his pious book of Emblem poetry was to Whitney's. Thus, a tradition that had begun at the dawn of the Renaissance as an attempt to recover the "sacred language of the gods" now closed with a book of homilies for the humbler classes that endeavored, Polonial-fashion, to point a moral and adorn a platitude.

The revulsion against Emblem poetry, and all it stood for, inevitably grew deeper during the positivist and deist Age of Enlightenment. One of its chief luminaries, the Earl of Shaftesbury, in his *Second Characters, or The Language of Forms,* published in 1713, there buried it under a heap of stony epithets, such as "enigmatical, preposterous, disproportionate, gouty and lame, impotent, pretentious, Egyptian, magical, mystical, monkish, and"—most crushing of all at the time—"gothic." And yet, for all that, reprints of Quarles and Withers as well as translations of foreign Emblem poets, such as the Dutch Jacob Cats, appeared from time to time; and Cesare Ripa's great *Iconologia,* republished in various editions throughout the century, still served as a source of symbolic imagery for painters and engravers. But Hermes himself—at least in his manifestation as Hermes Trismegistus—had apparently gone into a disappearing act that would last forever.

Or so it seemed. Under the spell of the hermetic philosophy, still potent even in that skeptical age, the visionary poet Christopher Smart (whose fragmentary epic, *Rejoice in the Lamb,* was written while he was confined in a madhouse) sought to reconcile the breach between spiritual and material reality, the Word and the Work, brought about by Newtonian science. Robert Browning, who rediscovered Smart's poetry, wrote of him in homage that he had "pierced the screen/Twixt word and thing"; and Smart, in his *Rejoice in the Lamb,* said of himself: "For my talent is to give an impression upon words by punching, that when the reader casts his eye upon 'em, he takes up the image from the mold which I have made." The same "talent," in essence, was shared by Smart's kindred spirit and true successor, William Blake, who also sought to recover the "Holy Word"

> That might controll
> The starry pole,
> And fallen, fallen light renew!

Blake's *The Gates of Paradise,* the centerpiece in our *Gallery,* was first conceived by him in 1793, when he gave it the subtitle *For Children;* but in 1818, toward the end of his creative life, he made several minor improvements in the emblems and added the

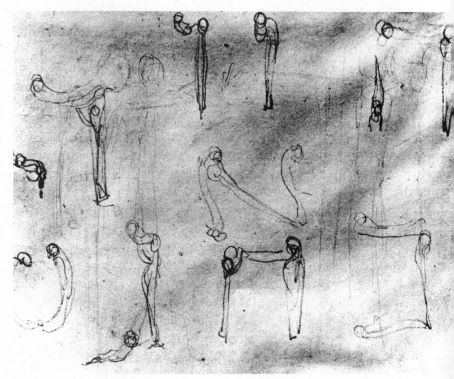

In 1803, while Blake was studying Hebrew, he experimented with composing Hebrew characters from human figures. The above attempt at a mystical anthropography was sketched on the reverse side of a drawing on the theme "War and the Fear of Invasion."

(Figure 5)

epigrammatic poem that unites them all, at which time he changed the subtitle to *For the Sexes.* Not only does *The Gates of Paradise* sum up his own career as a picture-poet, but it consummates the genre of Emblem poetry as well. The lowly social and aesthetic status to which it had declined suited his alchemical genius for transmuting base into high forms of art, as he had already demonstrated in making the *Songs of Innocence and of Experience* out of the plain speech and tic-toc meters of London street ballads and church hymnals.

The mystical ideas imagined and inscribed on *The Gates of Paradise* were, as we know, the distillation of his lifelong study of occult literature, such as the Cabala and the *Corpus Hermeticum,* the works of Paracelsus, Cornelius Agrippa, Robert Fludd, Jacob Boehme, Swedenborg, and the rest. In the self-esteemed Age of Reason these were dangerous ideas: for though religious heretics and ecstatics, ranters and necromancers, were no longer burned at the stake, as was the sixteenth-century Magus Giordano Bruno, they still ran the risk of being clapped into Bedlam. ("If Blake had a crack," wrote his disciple Samuel Palmer, "it was a crack that let the light through.") Blake's mysticism, regarded by others as religious frenzy and/or poetic madness, was what he himself referred to as "vision," that druidic faculty of "into-it-iveness" possessed by the prophets and seers of ancient times. "I rest not from my great task," he declared, not without a certain Churchillian grandiloquence,

To open the Eternal Worlds, to open the immortal Eyes
Of Man inwards into the Worlds of Thought, into Eternity
Ever expanding in the Bosom of God, the Human Imagination.

Toward the end of his life, in the 1820s, the painters Samuel Palmer and Edward Calvert and other admirers in a group calling themselves the "Shoreham Ancients" formed a charmed circle around the poet; but for the rest of the century and almost up to our own time, his work, except for several of his early lyrics, remained largely unknown.

By his original subtitle to *The Gates of Paradise,* namely, *For Children,* Blake of course did not mean that it was intended solely for them, but rather for all who had to become as such, in order to pass through "The Gates." Ironically, this subtitle turned out to be prophetic in a way he could not have foreseen. For the two most important picture-poets to appear in the later nineteenth century, Edward Lear and Lewis Carroll, for whom the play of the imagination was as profoundly serious as even their most profound ideas were playful, did conceive their books expressly for them.

> The Child's Toys & the Old Man's Reasons
> Are the Fruits of the Two Seasons,

wrote Blake in his "Auguries of Innocence." The magical potential of names and images to conjure up what they represent—*"Rumpelstiltskin!"*—seems to children of whatever historical epoch or society as much in the nature of things as such names once did universally to primitive man. Lear's totemic fantasies and Carroll's metalogical trip through the looking-glass thus belong to the same once-upon-a-time mythopoeic Dream Time. No wonder, then, that the only other eminent Victorian author of children's books who deserves comparison with them, Robert Louis Stevenson, was also to take up the by now almost forgotten form of Emblem poetry, if merely and mischievously to parody it, with the type of humor that has since become known as "black." (Dr. Jekyll might have composed the sentimental lyrics of Stevenson's *A Child's Garden of Verses,* Mr. Hyde his *Moral Emblems.*) But even this flickering revival of the hermetic spirit indicated that the god was abroad once more.

In France about this time, where the modernist movement in art and poetry was already under way, there could be no doubt. Following Baudelaire, the Symbolist poets, who revered him as a kind of Magus, took as their own credo his metaphorical conception of reality as a "forest of correspondences"; which conception, of course, itself corresponded to the one conceived long ago by the neoplatonist and hermetic philosophers. But for Baudelaire both parts of his metaphor had equal weight: it was a *forest,* one in which mankind was lost, not a metaphysical highway (or *circuitus spiritualis,* as Ficino called it) paved with logic that led from *ergo* to *ergo* straight to the Mind of God. Rimbaud, who hoped by such correspondences to discover for himself *"l'alchimie poétique,"* acclaimed Baudelaire as "the first see-er," a poet able "to inspect the invisible and to hear the unheard"; but then he added that "his much-praised form is a poor thing. Inventions of unknownness demand new forms." However, it was not the "wild" Rimbaud (*"un mystique à l'état sauvage,"* as Claudel once described him), but his temperamental opposite, the milquetoast mandarin Mallarmé, who was destined to invent these new forms. A correspondence of sorts exists, after all, between the petasus and caduceus of Hermes, the conical hat and hazel wand of a Renaissance Magus, and the tasseled nightcap and cigar of Mallarmé.

Mallarmé had based his own poetic faith, from which he never wavered, on another of Baudelaire's oracular pronouncements: "There is in the Word something sacred which prohibits us from making it into a game of chance." A poem therefore had to be no less than an ikon of the Absolute, with all the density, mystery, and inevitability of a "thing in itself." From his early "L'Après-Midi d'un Faune" to the baffling sonnets of his later years, the progressive obscurity of his style ensued from this lifelong effort to fix his vision of the Word into poetry that, no matter how self-referential and sealed from within, kept escaping into mere words.

In 1897, a year before his death, he published his most orphic and original poem, *Un Coup de Dés* (*A Throw of Dice*). At the time it first appeared in the Paris revue *Cosmopolis,* the young André Gide, awe-struck, called it "the farthest point to which the human spirit has yet ventured"; and Mallarmé himself—who would refer to it, only half-humorously, as "The Book"—believed that he had created a new kind of visual poetry: "words led back to their origin, the twenty-four letters of the alphabet, so gifted with infinity that they will finally consecrate language."

If God, as Einstein once said, refused to "play dice with the universe," neither would Mallarmé do so with the Word. *Un Coup de Dés,* in point and in fact, was a literary *coup d'état* designed not merely to change the rules but to abolish the "game" itself, in which poetry, by definition, could be no more than a "miscellany of chance inspirations." This meant, first of all, that its basic unit, the line, had to be annulled. "Let us have an end," he wrote in an essay called "The Book: A Spiritual Instrument," published in 1895, "to those incessant, back-and-forth motions of our eyes, traveling from one line to the next and beginning all over again": furrow after furrow, that the poet, plodding behind an earth-bound blinkered Pegasus, foot by foot, had previously laboriously sown with his *logoi spermatikoi.* What he proposed instead, and realized in *Un Coup de Dés,* was that the whole page—or, rather, the double-page spread—become the unit of the poem. The various

motifs, or idea-images, each represented by its own peculiar type-
face and surrounded like star-clusters by a "white silence," would
thus have the simultaneity of a picture and yet unfold from page to
page in a musical sequence. In the by-now classic typographical
version of *Un Coup de Dés,* published by *La Nouvelle Revue
Française* in 1914, the dismembered sentences, phrases scattered
throughout here and there, isolated words dangling in midpage,
like exposed nerve ends that are related and joined to one another
by synaptic cross-currents of meaning and metaphorical sidelights,
seem to comprise an uncanny X-ray photo, in words, of Mallarmé's
mind in the process of composing his poem.

Un Coup de Dés has remained a unique, and uniquely in-
scrutable, work, with many talmudic exegeses and commentaries
over the years but no successors in poetry. The "game," as Mal-
larmé had termed it, went on as before. For Guillaume Apollinaire,
the most innovative French poet of his era, *Un Coup de Dés* must
have served as the baptismal font for his own typographical picture-
poems published in *Calligrammes* in 1918. And, of course, James
Joyce, who also attempted like Mallarmé ("My shemblable! My
freer!") to write "The Book," begorra, in *Finnegans Wake,* rec-
ognized in his poem its only rival. ("But jig jog jug as Day the
Dicebox Throws, whang, loyal six I lead.") Yet the great Pascalian
wager made by Mallarmé on the formal structure of his picture-
poem—or, rather, moving picture-moving poem, like the unwind-
ing scroll of a Chinese landscape—that it would "consecrate
language," has, as said before, found no takers among other poets.

What was already a strong oriental current in art at the time of
Mallarmé, evident in the paintings of Whistler, Manet, and others
of the post-Impressionist school, now entered the mainstream of
Western poetry as well. By the year 1912 the Imagist movement,
led by Ezra Pound in London, had begun its reconstruction of
English poetics according to principles derived from Pound's study
of Chinese and Japanese forms, which he knew, however, only in
translation. The *haiku,* especially, assumed a paradigmatic impor-
tance for Imagism

IN A STATION OF THE METRO
The apparition of these faces in the crowd;
Petals on a wet, black bough.

comparable to that of the epigram for Emblem poetry. "The point of Imagism," Pound wrote, "is that it does not use images as *orna-ments*. The image is itself the speech." Furthermore, the "Image" —exalted by him this way and enshrined in quotes—not only "presents an intellectual and emotional complex in an instant of time," but also "is real because we know it directly." It had to be, then, the very dingdong *ding an sich* of poetry. The Imagist credo was reechoed in the United States some years later by Wallace Stevens: "The poem is the cry of its occasion, part of the *res* itself and not about it." And, expressed most succinctly, it became W. C. Williams's slogan: "No ideas but in things."

Pound, as T. S. Eliot said of him, is "the inventor of Chinese poetry for our time": not entirely out of whole cloth, though he was incapable of reading the poems of Li Po in the original, but by reworking the notes and glosses on them made around the turn of the century by the sinologist Ernest Fenollosa—who was himself dependent for his interpretations on a Japanese tutor—into the "translations" published as *Cathay* in 1915. The confusion that inevitably resulted was further compounded by the fact that Chinese characters contain no indications of number, tense, and gender; that Fenollosa often misunderstood—or else his tutor misunderstood—their meaning; and that Pound, in turn, sometimes misread Fenollosa's notes or else arbitrarily supplied his own versions. He therefore, as the French say, "Robinsonized" (adopting Rimbaud's noun-verb derived from the famous castaway who remade a barren island into a bit of seventeenth-century England), by transforming the—to him—virgin territory of Chinese poetry into a *chinoiserie* that was a replica of his own Symbolist and Imagist poetics. But in the process (as Pound so stated some fifty years later) he "gathered from the air a live tradition"—Western, of course, not Chinese—and forged the complex pictorial style of the *Cantos*.

As Fenollosa's literary executor, Pound also inherited his notes and papers for a lecture on Chinese ideograms, which he then incorporated into an essay, first published in *The Little Review* in 1919, entitled "The Chinese Written Character as a Medium for Poetry." And this, too, was destined to have an unforeseen effect on the course of modern literature.

"A true noun," wrote Fenollosa, "an isolated thing, does not exist in Nature. . . . Neither can a pure verb, an abstract motion, be possible in Nature. The eye sees noun and verb as one: things in motion, motion in things, and so the Chinese conception tends to represent them." He then cited several examples, e.g.: "The sun underlying the bursting forth of plants=spring"; or, " 'Boat' plus 'water'=boat-water: a ripple"; and so forth. Ergo, he concluded, "Chinese notation is something more than arbitrary symbols: it is based upon a vivid shorthand picture of the operations of Nature. . . . In reading Chinese we do not seem to be juggling mental counters, but to be watching *things* work out their fate." *(Fig. 6)*

Written to the tune
P'u-sa Man ("Bodhisatva Barbarians")
by Wei Chang (836?-910)

人 人 盡 說 江 南 好
遊 人 只 合 江 南 老
　 　 春 水 碧 於 天
　 　 畫 船 聽 雨 眠

爐 邊 人 似 月
皓 腕 凝 霜 雪
未 老 莫 還 鄉
還 鄉 須 斷 腸

Jen-jen chin shuo Chiang-nan hao
Man-man all say River-south good
Yu jen chih ho Chiang-nan lao
Wandering man only fit River-south old
Ch'un shuei pi yü t'ien
Spring water bluer than sky
Hua ch'uan t'ing yü mien
Painted boat hear rain sleep

Lu pien jen ssŭ yueh
Wine-jar side person like moon
Hao wan ning shuang hsüeh
Bright wrist frozen frost snow
Wei lao mo huan hsiang
Not-yet old do-not return home
Huan hsiang hsü tuan ch'ang
Return home must break bowels

Everyone is full of praise for the beauty of the South:
What can I do but end my days an exile in the South?
　　The spring river is bluer than the sky;
　　As it rains, in a painted barge I lie.

　　Bright as the moon is she who serves the wine;
　　Like frost or frozen snow her white wrists shine.
　　I'm not old yet: let me not depart!
　　For going home will surely break my heart!

(Figure 6)

So there it is, once more, the primal uroboric serpent biting its own tail. Though Chinese characters, like Egyptian hieroglyphs, must have originated as simple pictograms, they, too, evolved in the course of time into far more sophisticated phonetic symbols. Only a very small percentage are still directly representational. But by focusing almost exclusively on the pictorial aspect of the ideogram, Fenollosa (and Pound, too, as a result) muted its equally significant aural component, "the cry of its occasion." With a visionary enthusiasm that recalls that of Ficino and the other Renaissance hermetists when they first discovered Horapollo's *Hieroglyphika,* he declared, "Such a pictorial method, whether the Chinese exemplified it or not, would be *the ideal language of the world.*" (Editor's italics.)*

Dr. J. Y. Liu, in his *The Art of Chinese Poetry,* asserts:

> There is a fallacy still common among Western readers . . . that *all* Chinese characters are pictograms or ideograms. Ernest Fenollosa stressed this misconception and admired . . . their alleged pictorial qualities. While one is flattered by his attribution of superior poetic qualities to one's mother tongue . . . his conclusions are often incorrect, largely due to his refusal to recognize the phonetic element of Chinese characters. . . . As an introduction to Chinese poetry, the Fenollosa approach is, to say the least, seriously misleading.

Still, by being misled down this fork in the garden path—no doubt with Hermes showing the way in the gloaming—the followers of Ezra Pound, who himself followed Fenollosa, arrived in turn at the conception of what has become known as Concrete poetry.

The name was adopted, in 1955, after a meeting between the Brazilian poet Decio Pignatari and the Swiss but Bolivian-born poet Eugen Gomringer at Ulm in south Germany—the sister city, by the way, of Augsburg, where Alciati's first book of Emblem poetry was published—at which time they also agreed on a com-

---

* It should be mentioned that Fenollosa shared this belief with some illustrious company in the past. At the time when Europe was becoming aware, through the reports of Jesuit missionaries in China, that a living hieroglyphical language was in use by the Chinese, Francis Bacon (in the *Advancement of Learning,* VI, 1) expressed the hope that "real, not nominal, characters, to express, not . . . letters or words, but things and notions" might also be employed in Europe. And in the seventeenth century, the author of the *Pseudodoxia Epidemica,* Sir Thomas Browne, as well as the German philosopher and coinventor of the calculus, Wilhelm Leibniz, thought likewise.

The stone rubbing (*above left*) from an ancient Han tomb in China shows the serpent-tailed god Fu-Hsi, holding a set-square, entwined with his wife Nun-Kua, who is holding compasses. Fu-Hsi, the Chinese counterpart of Hermes Trismegistus-Thoth in Egypt, is said to have invented the eight trigrams from which Chinese characters later developed. According to the *I Ching:* "In the beginning there was as yet no moral nor social order. . . . Then came Fu-Hsi and looked upward and contemplated the images in the heavens, and looked downward and contemplated the occurrences on earth. He united man and wife, regulated the five stages of change, and laid down the laws of humanity. He then devised the eight trigrams in order to gain mastery over the world." Another legend claims that it was on the back of a tortoise shell—which, coincidentally, also served as the frame for the seven-stringed lyre of Hermes—where Fu-Hsi first discovered the sacred trigrams. The drawing by Holbein (*above right*) depicts Hermes's caduceus, a winged rod around which two serpents are convolved in an open figure 8, which gave him theurgic powers to join or separate all things. The universal "binding" principle, apotheosized as Fu-Hsi and Hermes, thus also connects East and West, a twain supposed never to meet; and yet (as Shakespeare wrote in *The Phoenix and the Turtle*) "how true a twain/ Seemeth this concordant one." *(Figure 7)*

mon program for what was already an international movement. Pignatari, together with the poets Augusto and Haroldo de Campos, had founded a magazine in 1952 in São Paulo, Brazil, called *Noigandres,* a name derived from a Provençal word of obscure provenance used by Arnaut Daniel and mentioned in one of Pound's *Cantos* ("Noigandres, eh, *noi*gandres, / Now what the DEFFIL can that mean!"), whose baffling signification, they must have felt, suited a kind of poetry that had not yet defined its scope. Gomringer, setting his sights through Mallarmé's *Un Coup de Dés,* had originally called his own ideographic poems "constellations." But the new name Concrete, thus fixed, became part of the *res* itself.

As one of its best-known practitioners as well as its chief theoretician, Gomringer conceived of Concrete poetry as a "tension of thing-words in space-time" that presented a simultaneous image-idea. By grasping the identity of this image-idea ("Single nature's double name"), and thus sharing mentally in its re-creation, the reader-viewer would experience a momentary arrest, or double-take, like the flash of insight followed by intellectual comprehension that occurs in solving a riddle. And a riddle, unriddled, is a metaphor whose terms, so to speak, have been "spelled" out. In that sense, therefore, the term Concrete poetry may be a misnomer, an instance of what the philosopher Whitehead once called the "fallacy of misplaced concreteness," for its source lies not in any Einsteinian "space-time" but in

> The Mind, that Ocean where each kind
> Does streight its own resemblance find,

as Andrew Marvell once wrote.

During the five hundred years that separate the picture-poems at either end of this *Gallery,* Emblem and Concrete, the idea of the visual symbol, which is the symbol itself as idea, has undergone a Circean metamorphosis. As perceived by modern depth psychology, the symbol not only has a rational side but a sensuous, figurative component as well that (according to Jung) is "inaccessible to reason, since it is composed . . . of the irrational data of pure inward and outward perception." So then, to bring this Introduction round as well, the *logoi spermatikoi* of neoplatonism have apparently made another descent, historically and psychologically: from the spirit, as metaphysical essences, down to the human consciousness, as logical forms and categories, then down once more to the undermind, as primordial archetypes and ghostly eidolons.

Finally, let me add that in extending the range of SPEAKING PICTURES: *A Gallery of Pictorial Poetry* to include cartoons, collages, sculpture, and even graffiti, my intention has been to exhibit whatever might conceivably fall under the spell of Hermes. "The aim of the poet," wrote Giambattista Marino, "is the marvelous"—that is, to enlarge the imagination the way light expands the eye.

*　　*　　*

Author's Note

The author would like to express his gratitude to those who in various ways helped to make this book possible: Harry Shefter, Laurie Brown, and Claudia Turner, of Washington Square Press (Simon & Schuster); Janet Fish, Jonathan Williams, and Richard Kostelanetz; Bruce Harris, Murray Schwartz, Linda Sunshine, Nancy Crow, and Frank Colosa, of Harmony Books (Crown Publishers, Inc.).

SPEAKING PICTURES

A Gallery of Pictorial Poetry
from the Sixteenth Century
to the Present

GEOFFREY WHITNEY
from *A Choice of Emblemes*

Hercules

While HERCULES with mighty club in hand
In lion's skin did sleep, and take his ease:
About him straight approach'd the Pygmies' band,
And for to kill this conqueror assays;
    But foolish dwarves: their force was all too small,
    And when he wak'd, like gnats he crush'd them all.

This warneth us that nothing past our strength
We should attempt: nor any work pretend
Above our power: lest that with shame at length
We weaklings prove, and faint before the end.
    The poor, that strive with mighty, this doth blame:
    And sots, that seek the learnèd to defame.

This emblem of the sleeping Hercules surrounded and attacked by pygmies was to undergo a sea-change in the memory of Jonathan Swift, reemerging as Lemuel Gulliver, Esq., seized and bound by the Lilliputians.

Sisyphus

Lo SISYPHUS, that rolls the restless stone
To top of hill, with endless toil, and pain:
Which being there, it tumbleth down alone,
And then the wretch must force it up again:
    And as it falls, he makes it still ascend;
    And yet no toil can bring this work to end.

This SISYPHUS: presenteth Adam's race.
The restless stone: their travail, and their toil:
The hill doth show the day, and eek the space,
Wherein they still do labor, work, and moil.
    And though till night they strive the hill to climb,
    Yet up again, the morning next betime.

Narcissus

NARCISSUS loved, and likèd so his shape,
He died at length with gazing there upon:
Which shows self-love, from which there few can scape,
A plague too rife: bewitcheth many a one.
 The rich, the poor, the learned, and the sot,
 Offend therein: and yet they see it not.

This makes us judge too well of our deserts
When others smile our ignorance to see:
And why? Because self-love doth wound our hearts,
And makes us think our deeds alone to be.
 Which secret sore lies hidden from our eyes,
 And yet the same an other plainly sees.

What folly more, what dotage like to this?
And do we so our own devise esteem?
And can we see so soon an other's miss?
And not our own? O blindness most extreme!
 Affect not then, but try, and prove thy deeds,
 For of self-love, reproach and shame proceeds.

Astronomer (Thales)

Th' ASTRONOMER by night beheld the stars to
    shine:
And what should chance an other year began for to
    divine.
But while too long in skies the curious fool did dwell,
As he was marching through the shade, he slipt into a
    well.
Then crying out for help, had friends at hand, by
    chance;
And now his peril being past, they thus at him do
    glance.
What foolish art is this (quoth they) thou hold'st so
    dear,
That thou foreshow the perils far: but not the dangers
    near?

The sixth-century-B.C. Greek philosopher Thales, who first
discovered the path of the sun from one end of the ecliptic
to the other, also has the distinction of being known as the
first "absentminded professor." According to Diogenes Laer-
tius: "He was once led out of his house by an old woman
for the purpose of observing the stars, and he fell into a
ditch and bewailed himself, upon which the old woman said,
'Do you, O Thales, who cannot see what is under your feet,
think that you shall understand what is in heaven?'"

Prometheus

To Caucasus, behold PROMETHEUS chain'd,
Whose liver still a greedy gripe doth rent:
He never dies, and yet is always pain'd
With tortures dire: by which the poets meant
    That he, that still amid misfortunes stands,
      Is sorrow's slave and bound in lasting bands.

For when that grief doth grate upon our gall,
Or surging seas, of sorrows most do swell,
That life is death, and is no life at all,
The liver rent, it doth the conscience tell:
    Which being launch'd, and prick'd, with inward care,
      Although we live, yet still we dying are.

Hamlet's universal self-debate on the racking question, "To
be, or not to be . . ./Whether 'tis nobler in the mind to suf-
fer/The slings and arrows of outrageous fortune,/Or to take
arms against a sea of troubles,/And by opposing end
them?," may well have had its source in Whitney's image of
"surging seas, of sorrows most do swell,/That life is death,
and is no life at all. . . ." It was Thales again, incidentally,
who asserted that "to be, or not to be" made no difference.
According to Diogenes Laertius: "Why then," said someone
to him, "do you not die?" "Because," said he, "it makes no
difference."

Mezentius

The tyrant vile MEZENTIUS put in ure
Amongst the plagues wherewith he murdered men:
To bind the quick and dead together sure,
And then to throw them both into a den.
　　Whereas the quick should still the dead embrace,
　　Until with pine he turned into that case.

Those wedding webs, which some do weave with ruth,
As when the one with strange disease doth pine:
Or when as age be coupled unto youth,
And those that hate enforcèd are to join,
　　This represents: and doth those parents show
　　Are tyrants mere who join their children so.

Yet many are who not the cause regard,
The birth, the years, nor virtues of the mind:
For gold is first with greedy men prefer'd,
And love is last, and liking set behind:
　　But parents hard, that matches make for goods,
　　Can not be free from guilt of children's bloods.

John Milton, in **The Doctrine and Discipline of Divorce** (1643), wrote of an incompatible husband and wife who ". . . instead of being one flesh, they will be rather two carcasses chained unnaturally together; or, as it may happen, a living soul bound to a dead corpse." Whitney's emblem of Mezentius must have seemed to Milton to symbolize his own conjugal miseries. The torture invented by Mezentius is described in Virgil's **Aeneid** (Book VIII).

Sirens

With pleasant tunes the SIRENS did allure
Ulysses wise to listen to their song:
But nothing could his manly heart procure,
He sailed away and scap'd their charming strong,
   The face he liked: the nether part, did loath:
   For woman's shape and fish's had they both.

Which shows to us, when Beauty seeks to snare
The careless man, who doth no danger dread,
That he should fly, and should in time beware,
And not on looks his sickly fancy feed:
   Such Mermaids live that promise only joys:
   But he that yields at length him self destroys.

Occasion (Opportunity)

What creature thou? *OCCASION I do show.*
On whirling wheel declare why dost thou stand?
Because I still am tossèd to and fro.
Why dost thou hold a razor in thy hand?
   That men may know I cut on every side,
   And when I come, I armies can divide.

But wherefore hast thou wings upon thy feet?
To show how light I fly with little wind.
What means long locks before? *That such as meet,*
May hold at first when they OCCASION find.
   Thy head behind all bald, what tells it more?
   That none should hold that let me slip before.

Why dost thou stand within an open place?
That I may warn all people not to stay,
But at the first, OCCASION to embrace,
And when she comes to meet her by the way.
   Lysippus so did think it best to be,
   Who did devise my image, as you see.

Leonardo da Vinci, who invented numerous emblems and allegorical figures, wrote in his **Notebooks:** "When fortune comes, seize her with a firm hand—in front, I counsel you, for behind she is bald." Whence the expression: "Seize time by the forelock." But the fourth-century-B.C. sculptor Lysippus, as Whitney points out in his poem, is said to have been the first to have conceived this device.

The Traveling Man

THE TRAVELING MAN, uncertain where to go
When divers ways before his face did lie,
Mercurius then the perfect path did show,
Which when he took, he never went awry,
    But to his wish his journey's end did gain
    In happy hour, by his direction plain.

This TRAVELING MAN doth tell our wandering state,
Before whose face, and eke on every side,
Bypaths, and ways, appear amid our gate,
That if the Lord be not our only guide
    We stumble, fall, and daily go astray:
    Then happy those whom God doth show the way.

GEORGE PUTTENHAM
from *The Arte of English Poesie*

A great Emperor in Tartary who they call *Can,* for
his good fortune in the wars & many notable conquests
he had made, was surnamed *Temir Cutzclewe;* this man
loved the Lady *Kermesine,* who presented him returning
from the conquest of *Corasoon* (a great kingdom ad-
joyning) with this *Lozange* made in letters of rubies &
diamants entermingled thus:

Sound
O Harpe
Shril lie out
Temir the ſtout
Rider who with sharpe
Trenching blade of bright ſteele
Hath made his fierceſt foes to feele
All ſuch as wrought him shame or harme
The ſtrength of his braue right arme,
Cleauing hard downe vnto the eyes
The raw skulles of his enemies,
Much honor hath he wonne
By doughtie deedes done
In Cora ſoon
And all the
Worlde
Round.

To which Can Temir *answered in* Fuzie, *with letters
of Emeralds and Ametists artificially cut and enter-
mingled, thus:*

Fiue
Sore batailes
Manfully fought
In blouddy fielde
With bright blade in hand
Hath Temir won & forſt to yeld
Many a Captaine ſtrong and ſtoute
And many a king his Crowne to vayle,
Conquering large countreys and land,
Yet ne uer wanne I vi ſto rie,
I ſpeake it to my greate glo rie,
So deare and ioy full vn to me,
As when I did firſt con quere thee
O Kerme ſine, of all myne foes
The moſt cruell, of all myne woes
The ſmarteſt, the ſweeteſt
My proude Con quest
My ri cheſt pray
O once a daye
Lend me thy ſight
Whoſe only light
Keepes me
Aliue.

Her Maieſtie, for many parts in her moſt noble and vertuous nature to be found, reſembled to the ſpire. Ye muſt begin beneath according to the nature of the deuice

From God the fountaine of all good, are deriued into the world all good things: and vpon her maieſtie all the good fortunes any worldly creature can be furniſht with. Reade downward according to the nature of the deuice.

        Skie. 1

      Azurd 2
      in the
      aſſurde,

    And better,
    And richer,
    Much greter,

  Crown & empir
  After an hier
  For to aſpire 4
  Like flame of fire
  In forme of ſpire

  To mount on hie,
  Con ti nu al ly
  With trauel & teen
  Moſt gratious queen
  Ye haue made a vow 5
  Shews vs plainly how
  Not fained but true,
  To euery mans vew,
  Shining cleere in you
  Of ſo bright an hewe,
  Euen thus vertewe

  Vanish out of our ſight
  Till his fine top be quite
  To Taper in the ayre 6
  Endeuors ſoft and ſaire
  By his kindly nature
  Of tall comely ſtature
  Like as this ſaire figure

   1 *God*
      On
      Hie
  2 *From*
     Aboue
  Sends loue,
  Wiſedome,
  Iu ſtice
  Cou rage,
  Boun tie,
  And doth geue
  Al that liue,
  Life & breath
  Harts eſe helth
  Childrē, welth
  Beauty ſtrēgth
  Reſtfull age,
  And at length
  A mild death,
  4 *He doeth beſtow*
  All mens fortunes
  Both high & low
  And the beſt things
  That earth cā haue
  Or mankind craue,
  Good queens & kings
  Fi nally is the ſame
  Who gaue you (madā)
  Seyſon of this Crowne
  With poure ſoueraigne
  5 *Impug nable right,*
  Redoubtable might,
  Moſt proſperous raigne
  Eternall re nowme,
  And that your chiefeſt is
  Sure hope of heauens blis.

These iconic poems from George Puttenham's **The Arte of English Poesie,** published in 1589, were cited by him as specimens of what he termed "ocular proportion." Puttenham was somehow under the impression that such poetry flourished in the courts of China, Tartary, and Persia, and urged English "courtly makers" to adopt the style. However, the late scholar and critic C. S. Lewis, who thought little of them, wrote in his **English Literature in the Sixteenth Century** that they resembled "the court poetry of Lilliput in the age of Gulliver."

Her Maieſtie reſembled to the crowned piller. Ye muſt read vpward.

Is bliſſe with immortalitie.
Her trymeſt top of all ye ſee,
Garniſh the crowne
Her iuſt renowne
Chapter and head,
Parts that maintain
And womanhead
Her mayden raigne
In te gri tie:
In ho nour and
With ve ri tie:
Her roundnes ſtand
Strēgthen the ſtate.
By their increaſe
With out de bate
Concord and peace
Of her ſup port,
They be the baſe
With ſtedfaſtneſſe
Vertue and grace
Stay and comfort
Of Al bi ons reſt,
The ſounde Pillar
And ſeene a farre
Is plainely expreſt
Tall ſtately and ſtrayt
By this no ble pour trayt

Philo to the Lady Calia, ſendeth this Odolet of her prayſe in forme of a Piller, which ye muſt read downeward.

Thy Princely port and Maieſtie
Is my ter rene dei tie,
Thy wit and ſence
The ſtreame & ſource
Of e lo quence
And deepe diſcours,
Thy faire eyes are
My bright loadſtarre,
Thy ſpeache a darte
Percing my harte,
Thy face a las,
My loo king glaſſe,
Thy loue ly lookes
My prayer bookes,
Thy pleaſant cheare
My ſunſhine cleare,
Thy ru full ſight
My darke midnight,
Thy will the ſtent
Of my con tent,
Thy glo rye flour
Of myne ho nour,
Thy loue doth giue
The lyfe I lyue,
Thy lyfe it is
Mine earthly bliſſe:
But grace & fauour in thine eies
My bodies ſoule & ſouls paradiſe.

JOHN DONNE
To Mr. George Herbert

SENT HIM WITH ONE OF MY SEALS OF THE ANCHOR
AND CHRIST.

A sheaf of snakes used heretofore to be my seal,
which is the crest of our poor family.

Adopted in God's family, and so
My old coat lost, into new arms I go.
The cross my seal in baptism spread below,
Does by that form into an anchor grow.
Crosses grow anchors, bear as thou shouldst do
Thy cross, and that cross grows an anchor too.
But he that makes our crosses anchors thus,
Is Christ, who there is crucified for us.
Yet with this I may my first serpents hold
(God gives new blessings, and yet leaves the old);
The serpent may, as wise, my pattern be,
My poison, as he feeds on dust, that's me.
And, as he rounds the earth to murder, sure
He is my death, but on the cross my cure.
Crucify nature then; and then implore
All grace from him, crucified there before.
When all is cross, and that cross anchor grown,
This seal's a catechism, not a seal alone.
Under that little seal great gifts I send,
Both works and prayers, pawns and fruits of a friend.
O may that saint that rides on our great seal,
To you that bear his name large bounty deal.

In Izaak Walton's **The Life of John Donne, D.D.,** published
in 1639, where Donne's Emblematic poem first appeared,
Walton wrote: "Betwixt this George Herbert and Dr. Donne
there was a long and dear friendship, made up of such a
sympathy of inclinations, that they coveted and joyed to be
in each other's company; and this happy friendship was still
maintained by many sacred endearments, of which that
which followeth [the poem] may be some testimony."

GEORGE HERBERT
The Altar

The Altar.

A broken A L T A R , Lord , thy ſervant reares
Made of a heart , and cemented with teares
   Whoſe parts are as thy hand did frame;
   No workmans tool hath touch'd the ſame.
      A H E A R T alone
      Is ſuch a ſtone
      As nothing but
      Thy pow'r doth cut.
      Wherefore each part
      Of my hard heart
      Meets in this frame,
      To praiſe thy name.
   That if I chance to hold my peace,
   Theſe ſtones to praiſe thee may not ceaſe.
O let thy bleſſed S A C R I F I C E be mine,
And ſanctifie this A L T A R to be thine.

Easter-wings

Easter wings.

Lord, who createdſt man in wealth and ſtore,
Though fooliſhly he loſt the ſame,
Decaying more and more,
Till he became
Moſt poore :
With thee
O let me riſe
As larks, harmoniouſly,
And ſing this day thy victories:
Then ſhall the fall further the flight in me.

Easter wings.

My tender age in ſorrow did beginne
And ſtill with ſickneſſes and ſhame
Thou didſt ſo puniſh ſinne,
That I became
Moſt thinne.
With thee
Let me combine,
And feel this day thy victorie :
For, if I imp my wing on thine,
Affliction ſhall advance the flight in me.

ROBERT HERRICK
The Pillar of Fame

The pillar of Fame.

FAmes pillar here, at laſt, we ſet,
   Out-during *Marble*, *Braſſe*, or *Jet*,
   Charm'd and enchanted ſo,
    As to withſtand the blow
       Of   overthrow :
       Nor ſhall the ſeas,
       Or Oᴜᴛʀᴀɢᴇs
       Of ſtorms orebear
       What we up-rear,
       Tho Kingdoms fal,
    This   pillar   never   ſhall
    Decline or waſte at all ;
But ſtand for ever by his owne
Firme and well fixt foundation.

TO his Book's end this laſt line he'd have
    plac't,
Jocond his Muſe was ; but his Life was chaſt.

FINIS.

ANONYMOUS
Love Knot

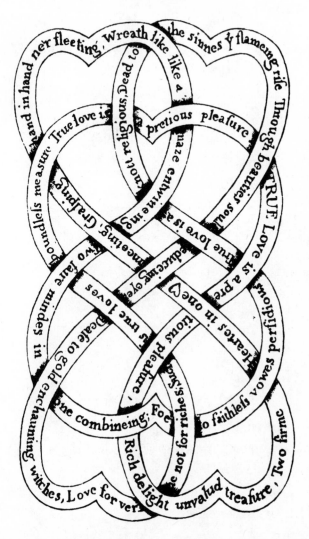

The above "Love Knot" and the other "fancies and fantasticks" that follow circulated throughout merry England even during the reign of Cromwell's Puritan "saints," taking their place alongside the books of Emblem poetry that offered spiritual guidance and moral uplift. They were first published in **Witt's Recreations** (1640) and **Musarum Deliciae: or, The Muses Recreation** (1656).

Rebus

The a

whilst

I  2 Lovers

That
gazed me.

There was nor

nor loathsome

That might disturb or break delight,

Nor nor

in that same road,
And yet to me they seemed affright.
favour
Then them I told,
True Love cannot be
bold

Those strange little creatures up there are, respectively, a flea and a toad.

Love Knot

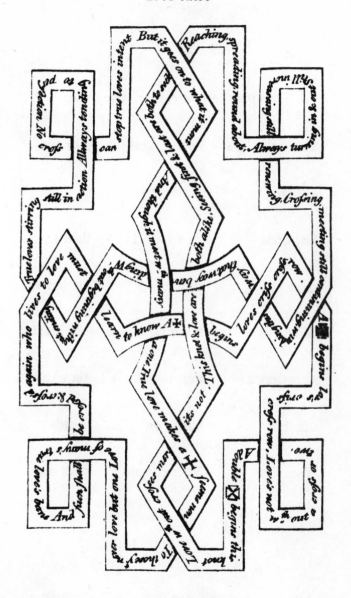

Acrostic

These may be read two or three wayes.

Your face	Your tongue	your wit
so faire	so smooth	so sharp
first drew	then mov'd	then knit
mine eye	mine eare	my heart
Mine eye	Mine eare	My heart
thus drawn	thus mov'd	thus knit
affects	hangs on	yeelds to
Your face	Your tongue	your wit

The third way, incidentally, goes from right to left and from left to right in alternate lines, in imitation of the ancient Greek manner of writing called **boustrophedon,** "as the ox turns in plowing."

Love Knot

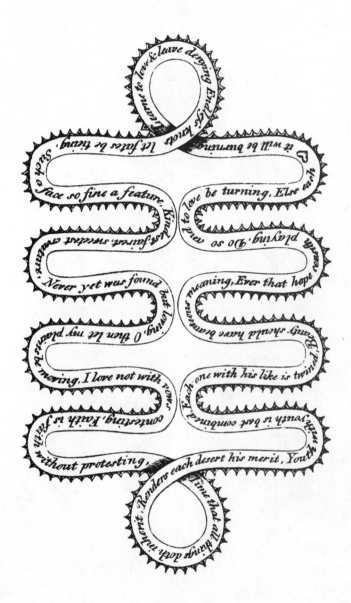

Rebus

If V 2 I, as I 2 V am true,

^I
V must lye, and

Thoughts———⎫
Searching——⎬ c
    Valued⎫
    Love———⎬ may   **B**

    Truth never ties
Too A foole yy

If have part   [heart W·R]

And [heart IF] V bb

Y'have 1. 2. many then I. C.
And R not worth

   Write⎫   QQ
I'le———⎬ not yours VV

The sharp bottom of the old-style letter V, once universally
employed by printers, has of course been rounded and
plumped out by time to become our own curvaceous U.

On Turn-coat

Passenger, Stay, Reade, Walk. Here Lyeth,

ANDREW TURNCOAT, WHO WAS NEITHER SLAVE, NOR SOULDIER, NOR PHYSITIAN, NOR FENCER, NOR COBLER, NOR FILCHER, NOR LAWYER, NOR USURER, BUT ALL; WHO LIVED NEITHER IN CITY, NOR COUNTREY, NOR AT HOME, NOR ABROAD, NOR AT SEA, NOR AT LAND, NOR HERE, NOR ELSEWHERE, BUT EVERY WHERE; WHO DIED NEITHER OF HUNGER, NOR POYSON, NOR HATCHET, NOR HALTER, NOR DOGGE, NOR DISEASE, BUT OF ALL TOGETHER. I. I. H. BEING NEITHER HIS DEBTOR, NOR HEIRE, NOR KINSMAN, NOR FRIEND, NOR NEIGHBOUR, BUT ALL, IN HIS MEMORY HAVE ERECTED, THIS NEITHER MONUMENT, NOR TOMB, NOR SEPULCHER, BUT ALL, WISHING NEITHER EVIL, NOR WEL, NEITHER TO THEE, NOR TO ME, NOR HIM, BUT ALL UNTO ALL.

HENRY PEACHAM
from *Minerva Britanna*

Melancholy

Here Melancholy, musing in his fits,
Pale visaged, of complexion cold and dry,
All solitary at his study sits
Within a wood, devoid of company
   Save Madge the owl, and melancholy Puss,
   Light-loathing creatures, hateful, ominous.

His mouth, in sign of silence, up is bound,
For Melancholy loves not many words;
One foot on cube is fixed upon the ground,
The which him plodding constancy affords;
   A sealèd purse he bears, to show no vice
   So proper is to him as avarice.

An accomplished artist as well as a poet, Peacham drew the
designs for these emblems and also wrote the accompanying
verses.

The Fool

This simple fool that here bestrides the bough,
And knowing well the danger underneath,
Yet busily doth saw the same in two,
Like idle ape, though to his present death:
    Which if he had foreborn, and let it grow,
    He free from harm had scaped the pikes below.

To this same idiot such we liken may
Of trusty friends as do not know the use,
But while they are their props and only stay
Will cut them off by this or that abuse,
    Or lose their favor by behavior ill,
    Who otherwise might have upheld them still.

The Cat and the Cock

The cat the cock held prisoner in her paw,
And said of birds he most deserved to die,
For that, contrary unto nature's law,
His kindred he abused incestuously—
    His mother, sisters—and a noise did keep
    With crowing still when others fain would sleep.

In his defence, "Hereto," replied the cock,
"My fault of lust is for my master's gain;
I am, for crowing, called the 'Plowman's clock,'
Whom I awake betime to daily pain."
    "No doubt," quoth Puss, "of reasons thou hast store,
    But I am fasting, and can hear no more."

Death and Cupid

Death meeting once with Cupid in an inn
Where room was scant, together both they lay.
Both weary (for they roving both had been),
Now on the morrow when they should away,
    Cupid Death's quiver at his back had thrown,
    And Death took Cupid's, thinking it his own.

By this o'ersight, it shortly came to pass
That young men died who ready were to wed;
And age did revel with his bonny lass,
Composing garlands for his hoary head.
    Invert not nature, O ye Powers twain,
    Give Cupid's darts, and Death take thine again.

BEN JONSON

An Explication of the Emblemes

A.   Here, like *Arion,* our *Coryate* doth draw
All sorts of fish with Musicke of his maw.

B.   Here, not up *Holdborne,* but downe a steepe hill,
Hee's carried 'twixt *Montrell* and *Abbevile.*

C.   A Horse here is sadled, but no *Tom* him to backe,
It should rather have bene *Tom* that a horse did lack.

D. Here up the *Alpes* (not so plaine as to *Dunstable*)
Hee's carried like a Cripple, from Constable to
Constable.

E. A *Punke* here pelts him with egs. How so?
For he did but kisse her, and so let her go.

F. Religiously here he bids, row from the *stewes,*
He will expiate this sinne with converting the *Jewes.*

G. And there, while he gives the zealous *Bravado,*
A *Rabbin* confutes him with the *Bastinado.*

H. Here, by a *Boore* too, hee's like to be beaten
For Grapes he had gather'd before they were eaten.

I. Old Hat here, torne Hose, with Shoes full of gravell,
And louse-dropping Case, are the *Armes* of his travell.

K. Here, finer then comming from his Punke you him see,
F. shewes what he was, K. what he will bee.

L. Here *France* and *Italy* both to him shed
Their hornes, and *Germany* pukes on his head.

M. And here he disdaind not, in a forraine land
To lie at Livory, while the Horses did stand.

N. But here, neither trusting his hands, nor his legs,
Beeing in feare to be robd, he most learnedly begs.

Thomas Coryat's famous **Crudities,** an account of the marvels and perils encountered on a journey through darkest Europe in 1610, was edited by his "poeticall friend Mr. Benjamin Johnson" (sic), and further embellished with mock-congratulatory verses to the author by Donne and Drayton, among others. The biographer, Thomas Fuller, once wrote of Coryat: "He carried folly (which the charitable called merriment) in his very face, the shape of his head being like a sugarloaf inverted, with the little end before, as composed of fancy and memory, without any common sense." Nonetheless, it was Coryat who most profoundly altered the taste of his own age and of future generations, for he first introduced the table fork from Italy into England, employing it without shame whenever he dined, even in public, though much ridiculed for his foreign affectations.

from *A Celebration of Charis*
The Triumph of Venus (Francesco del Cossa)

Her Triumph

See the Chariot at hand here of Love
    Wherein my Lady rideth!
Each that drawes, is a Swan, or a Dove,
    And well the Carre Love guideth;
As she goes, all hearts doe duty
      Unto her beauty;

And enamour'd, doe wish, so they might
          But enjoy such a sight,
That they still were, to run by her side,
Through Swords, through Seas, whether she would ride.

Doe but looke on her eyes, they doe light
    All that Loves world compriseth!
Doe but looke on her Haire, it is bright
    As Loves starre when it riseth!
Doe but marke her forhead's smoother
          Then words that sooth her!
And from her arched browes, such a grace
          Sheds it selfe through the face,
As alone there triumphs to the life
All the Gaine, all the Good, of the Elements strife.

Have you seene but a bright Lillie grow,
    Before rude hands have touch'd it?
Ha'you mark'd but the fall o'the Snow
    Before the soyle hath smutch'd it?
Ha'you felt the wooll of Bever?
          Or Swans Downe ever?
Or have smelt o'the bud o'the Brier?
          Or the Nard in the fire?
Or have tasted the bag of the Bee?
O so white! O so soft! O so sweet is she!

The "Charis" who inspired Ben Jonson's ecstatic tribute is believed to have been Elizabeth Hatton, widow of Sir William Hatton, whose name she kept after she was remarried to the famous jurist Sir Edward Coke in 1598. Lady Elizabeth, a court beauty, played the role of the goddess Venus in a masque by Jonson presented in 1608. As described by a contemporary: "The scene to this Masque was a high, steep, red cliff, advancing itself into the clouds. . . . Beyond the cliff was seen nothing but clouds, thick and obscure; till on the sudden, with a solemn music, a bright sky breaking forth, there were discovered first two doves, then two swans with silver geers, drawing forth a triumphal chariot; in which Venus sat, crowned with her star. . . ."

The emblem, on the same mythic theme, is from the great fresco by Francesco del Cossa, "The Triumph of Venus," at the Palazzo Schifanoia in Ferrara.

THOMAS CAMPION

The Embarkment for Cythera (Antoine Watteau)

Canto Secundo

What faire pompe have I spide of glittering Ladies;
With locks sparckled abroad, and rosie Coronet
On their yvorie browes, trackt to the daintie thies
With roabs like *Amazons,* blew as Violet,
With gold Aglets adornd, some in a changeable
Pale, with spangs wavering, taught to be moveable.

Then those Knights that a farre off with dolorous
      viewing
Cast their eyes hetherward: loe, in an agonie,
All unbrac'd, crie aloud, their heavie state ruing:
Moyst cheekes with blubbering, painted as *Ebonie*
Blacke; their feltred haire torne with wrathfull hand:
And whiles astonied, starke in a maze they stand.

But hearke, what merry sound! what sodaine harmonie!
Looke, looke neere the grove where the Ladies doe
    tread
With their knights the measures waide by the melodie!
Wantons, whose travesing make men enamoured!
Now they faine an honor, now by the slender wast
He must lift hir aloft, and seale a kisse in hast.

Streight downe under a shadow for wearines they lie
With pleasant daliance, hand knit with arme in arme;
Now close, now set aloof, they gaze with an equall eie,
Changing kisses alike; streight with a false alarme,
Mocking kisses alike, powt with a lovely lip.
Thus drownd with jollities, their merry daies doe slip.

But stay! now I discerne they goe on a Pilgrimage
Toward Loves holy land, faire *Paphos* or *Cyprus*.
Such devotion is meete for a blithesome age;
With sweet youth it agrees well to be amorous.
Let olde angrie fathers lurke in an Hermitage:
Come, weele associate this jollie Pilgrimage!

---

lines 3-4: trackt to . . . like Amazons: *with their tunics pulled up
to the thighs.* line 5: Aglets: *metallic laces.* line 6: Pale: *pall, or
cloak.* spangs: *spangles.* line 11: feltred: *disheveled.* line 15:
waide: *measured.* line 16: travesing: *movements.* line 17: faine
an honor: *bow.* line 18: lift her aloft: *the dance is the Volta.*
line 21: with an equall eie: *with the same intense gaze.* line 26:
Paphos or Cyprus: *where Venus had her shrine.* line 30: associate:
join.

This marvelously airy and harmonious poem by the young
Thomas Campion was probably composed and set to music
for a masque presented at Queen Elizabeth's court in 1591.
The theme of a voyage by lovers to the legendary isle of
Venus, which also inspired Watteau's **The Embarkment for
Cythera,** stems not from classical but from medieval tradi-
tion.

RICHARD CRASHAW

Saint Teresa and the Seraph (Giovanni Lorenzo Bernini)

from *A Hymn to Saint Teresa*

O how oft shalt thou complain
Of a sweet & subtle PAIN.
Of intolerable JOYES;
Of a DEATH, in which who dyes
Loves his death, and dyes again.
And would for ever so be slain.
And lives, & dyes; and knowes not why
To live, But that he thus may never leave to DY.
How kindly will thy gentle HEART
Kisse the sweetly-killing DART!
And close in his embraces keep
Those delicious Wounds, that weep
Balsam to heal themselves with.   Thus
When These thy DEATHS, so numerous,
Shall all at last dy into one,
And melt thy Soul's sweet mansion;
Like a soft lump of incense, hasted
By too hott a fire, & wasted
Into perfuming clouds, so fast
Shalt thou exhale to Heavn at last
In a resolving SIGH, and then
O what?   Ask not the Tongues of men.
Angells cannot tell, suffice,
Thy selfe shall feel thine own full joyes
And hold them fast for ever.   There
So soon as thou shalt first appear,
The MOON of maiden starrs, thy white
MISTRESSE, attended by such bright
Soules as thy shining self, shall come
And in her first rankes make thee room;
Where 'mongst her snowy family
Immortall wellcomes wait for thee.

Bernini's great statue of Saint Teresa in the throes of divine
love, and Crashaw's equally celebrated poem on the same
theme, were both inspired by a passage in her memoirs telling of her rapture during a mystical encounter with a seraph,
who plunged a flame-tipped golden arrow many times forcefully and rhythmically into her heart. As she wrote: "The
paine of it was so excessive, that it forced me to utter
groanes; and the suavitie, which that extremitie of paine
gave, was also so very excessive, that there was no desiring
at all, to be ridd of it. . . ."

FRANCIS QUARLES

Inopem me copia fecit.

*Ye may suck, but not be satisfied with the breast
of her consolation.*

Isaiah 66:2

What, never fill'd? Be thy lips screw'd so fast
  To th'earth's full breast? for shame, for shame,
      unseize thee;
Thou take'st a surfeit where thou should'st but taste,
  And make'st too much not half enough to please thee.
    Ah, fool, forbear; thou swallowest at one breath
Both food and poison down; thou draw'st both milk
      and death.

The ub'rous breasts, when fairly drawn, repast
  The thriving infant with their milky flood;
But, being overstrain'd, return at last
  Unwholesome gulps compos'd of wind and blood.
    A mod'rate use doth both repast and please;
Who strains beyond a mean, draws in and gulps disease.

But, O that mean, whose good the least abuse
   Makes bad, is too, too hard to be directed:
Can thorns bring grapes, or crabs a pleasing juice?
    There's nothing wholesome where the whole's
        infected.
      Unseize thy lips: earth's milk's a ripen'd core
That drops from her disease, that matters from her sore.

Think'st thou that paunch, that burlies out thy coat,
   Is thriving fat; or flesh, that seems so brawny?
Thy paunch is dropsy'd, and thy cheeks are bloat;
    Thy lips are white, and thy complexion tawny;
      Thy skin's a bladder blown with wat'ry tumors;
Thy flesh a trembling bog, a quagmire full of humors.

And thou, whose thriveless hands are ever straining
   Earth's fluent breasts into an empty sieve,
That always hast, yet always art complaining,
    And whin'st for more than earth hath pow'r to give;
      Whose treasure flows and flees away as fast;
That ever hast, and hast, yet hast not what thou hast.

What less than fool is man to prog and plot,
   And lavish out the cream of all his care,
To gain poor seeming goods, which, being got,
    Make firm possession but a thoroughfare;
      Or, if they stay, they furrow thoughts the deeper;
And, being kept with care, they lose their careful
        keeper!

The plates for Quarles's **Emblems** (1635) were taken from Herman Hugo's **Pia Desideria** (1624) and Phillippe de Mallery's **Typus Mundi** (1627). The engravings were by W. Marshall, W. Simpson, and John Payne.

O that they were wise, that they understood this, that
they would consider their latter end!

Deuteronomy 32:29

FLESH   SPIRIT

Fl.: What means my sister's eye so oft to pass
Thro' the long entry of that optic glass?
Tell me, what secret virtue doth invite
Thy wrinkled eye to such unknown delight?
  Sp.: It helps the sight, makes things remote appear
In perfect view; it draws the objects near.
  Fl.: What sense-delighting objects dost thou spy?
What doth that glass present before thine eye?
  Sp.: I see thy foe, my reconcilèd friend,
Grim death, ev'n standing at the glass' end:
His left hand holds a branch of palm; his right
Holds forth a two-edg'd sword. *Fl.:* A proper sight,
And is this all? Doth thy prospective please
Th'abused fancy with no shapes but these?

Sp.: Yes, I behold the darken'd sun bereav'n
Of all his light, the battlements of heav'n
Swelt'ring in flames; the angel-guarded Son
Of glory on his high tribunal throne;
I see a brimstone sea of boiling fire,
And fiends, with knotted whips of flaming wire,
Tort'ring poor souls, that gnash their teeth in vain,
And gnaw their flame-tormented tongues for pain. . . .
   Fl.: Can thy distemper'd fancy take delight
In view of tortures? These are shows t'affright:
Look in this glass triangular; look here,
Here's that will ravish eyes. *Sp.:* What seest thou there?
   Fl.: The world in colours; colours that disdain
The cheeks of Proteus, or the silken train
Of Flora's nymphs; such various sorts of hue,
As sun-confronting Iris never knew:
Here, if thou please to beautify a town,
Thou may'st; or, with a hand, turn't upside down;
Here may'st thou scant or widen by the measure
Of thine own will; make short or long at pleasure:
Here may'st thou tire thy fancy, and advise
With shows more apt to please more curious eyes.
   Sp.: Ah fool! that dote'st on vain, on present toys,
And disrespect'st those true, those future joys;
How strongly are thy thoughts befool'd, alas!
To dote on goods that perish with thy glass;
Nay, vanish with the turning of a hand!
Were they but painted colours, it might stand
With painted reason that they might devote thee;
But things that have no being to besot thee!
Foresight of future torments is the way
To balk those ills which present joys bewray.
As thou hast fool'd thyself, so now come hither,
Break that fond glass, and let's be wise together.

Debilitata fides : Terbras Astræa reliquit.

The devil is come unto you, having great power,
because he knoweth that he hath but a short time.

Revelation 12:12

Lord, canst thou see and suffer? Is thy hand
  Still bound to th'peace? Shall earth's black monarch
      take
A full possession of thy wasted land?
  O, will thy slumb'ring vengeance never wake,
  Till full-aged law-resisting custom shake
The pillars of thy right by false command?
    Unlock thy clouds, great Thund'rer, and come down,
    Behold whose temples wear thy sacred crown;
Redress, redress our wrongs; revenge, revenge thy own.

See how the bold usurper mounts the seat
   Of royal majesty; how overstrawing
Perils with pleasure, pointing ev'ry threat
   With bug-bear death, by torments overawing
   Thy frighted subjects; or by favours drawing
Their tempted hearts to his unjust retreat;
   Lord, canst thou be so mild, and he so bold?
   Or can thy flocks be thriving, when the fold
Is govern'd by the fox? Lord, canst thou see, and hold?

That swift-wing'd advocate, that did commence
   Our welcome suits before the King of kings,
That sweet embassador, that hurries hence
   What airs th'harmonious soul or sighs or sins,
   See how she flutters with her idle wings;
Her wings are clipt, and eyes put out by sense;
   Sense-conqu'ring faith is now grown blind and cold,
   And basely craven'd, that in times of old
Did conquer heav'n itself, do what th'Almighty could.

Behold, how double fraud does scourge and tear
   Astraea's wounded sides, plough'd up, and rent
With knotted cords, whose fury has no ear;
   See how she stands a pris'ner to be sent
   A slave into eternal banishment,
I know not whither; O, I know not where:
   Her patent must be cancel'd in disgrace;
   And sweet-lip'd fraud, with her divided face,
Must act Astraea's part, must take Astraea's place.

Faith's pinion's clipt, and fair Astraea gone!
   Quick-seeing Faith now blind, and Justice see:
Has Justice now found wings? And has Faith none?
   What do we here? Who would not wish to be
   Dissolv'd from earth, and with Astraea flee
From this blind dungeon to that sun-bright throne?
   Lord, is thy sceptre lost, or laid aside?
   Is hell broke loose, and all her fiends unty'd?
Lord, rise, and rouse, and rule, and crush their furious
     pride.

Ye are of your father the devil, and the lusts
of your father ye will do.

John 8:44

Here's your right ground: wag gently o'er this black:
　'Tis a short cast; y'are quickly at the jack.
Rub, rub an inch or two; two crowns to one
　On this bowl's side; blow, wind; 'tis fairly thrown:
The next bowl's worse that comes; come, bowl away:
　Mammon, you know the ground; untutor'd, play:
Your last was gone; a yard of strength, well spared,
　Had touch'd the block; your hand is still too hard.
Brave pastime, readers, to consume that day,
　Which, without pastime, flies too swift away!
See how they labour, as if day and night
　Were both too short to serve their loose delight:
See how their curved bodies wreath, and screw
　Such antic shapes as Proteus never knew:

One raps an oath, another deals a curse;
    He never better bowl'd; this, never worse:
One rubs his itchless elbow, shrugs and laughs:
    The other bends his beetle brows, and chafes:
Sometimes they whoop, sometimes their Stygian cries
    Send their black Santos to the blushing skies;
Thus mingling humours in a mad confusion,
    They make bad premises, and worse conclusion:
But where's a palm that Fortune's hand allows
    To bless the victor's honourable brows?
Come, reader, come; I'll light thine eye the way
    To view the prize, the while the gamesters play:
Close by the jack, behold, jill Fortune stands
    To wave the game; see in her partial hands
The glorious garland's held in open show,
    To cheer the lads, and crown the conqu'ror's brow.
The world's the jack; the gamesters that contend
    Are Cupid, Mammon: that judicious fiend
That gives the ground, is Satan: and the bowls
    Are sinful thoughts; the prize, a crown for fools.
Who breathes that bowls not? What bold tongue can
      say,
    Without a blush, he has not bowl'd today?
It is the trade of man, and ev'ry sinner
    Has play'd his rubbers: every soul's a winner.
The vulgar proverb's crost, he hardly can
    Be a good bowler and an honest man.
Good God! turn thou my Brazil thoughts anew;
    New-sole my bowls, and make their bias true.
I'll cease the game, till fairer ground be given,
Nor wish to win, until the mark be heav'n.

GEORGE WITHER
from *A Collection of Emblemes*

No Heart can thinke . . .

No Heart *can thinke, to what ſtrange ends,* *The* Tongues *unruely* Motion *tends.*

Well-worthy of our better Heeding were
That Holy Pen-man's Lesson, who hath said,
We should be slow to Speak, and swift to Hear,
If well the nature of the Tongue we weigh'd.
For, if we let it loose, it getteth Wings,
And flies with wanton Carelessness about;
It prateth in all places, of All things,
Tells Truth and Lies, and babbleth Secrets out.

To speak of things unknown it taketh leave,
As if it had all Knowledge in Possession;
And Mysteries (which no Man can conceive)
Are thought fit Objects for the Tongue's Expression.
With Truth it mixeth Errors; says, unsays;
And is the Preacher of all Heresies.
That Heart, which gives it motion, it betrays;
And utters Curses, Oaths, and Blasphemies.
It spreads all Slanders, which base Envy raiseth;
It moveth Anger, and begetteth Hates:
It blameth Virtue; filthy Deeds it praiseth;
And causeth Uproars, Murders, and Debates.
Yea, 'tis the chiefest Factor for the Devil;
And yet, with speeches feignedly-sincere,
It otherwhile reproveth what is Evil,
And will in Lowly-words a Saint appear.
   Now this is known; we, next of all, should learn,
How we may shun the Mischief being known;
How we bad Tongues, in Others, may discern;
And how to guide and moderate our Own.
    And reason good; for none can apprehend
    What Mischief doth an Evil Tongue attend.

A curious feature of Wither's **A Collection of Emblemes,**
published in 1635, was the inclusion of an index in the form
of a roulette chart, with a pointer for the reader to spin
around and so determine by chance, **I Ching** style, which
moral emblem applied at the time to himself. The engrav-
ings were by Crispyn van de Passe.

The Bees . . .

The Bees, will in an Helmet breed ;
And, Peace, doth after Warre, succeed.

When you have heeded, by your Eyes of sense,
This Helmet, hiving of a Swarm of Bees,
Consider what may gather'd be from thence,
And what your Eye of Understanding sees.
   That Helmet, and those other Weapons there,
Betoken War; the Honey-making flies,
An Emblem of a happy Kingdom are,
Enjoying Peace by painful Industries:
And when all these together are expressed,
As in this Emblem, where the Bees do seem
To make their dwelling in a Plumed-Crest,
A Moral is implied, worthy esteem.

For these infer, mysteriously, to me
That Peace, and Art, and Thrift most firm abides
In those Republics where Arms cherisht be,
And where true Martial discipline resides.
When, of their Stings, the Bees disarm'd become,
They who on others' Labours use to prey
Encourag'd are, with violence, to come
And bear their Honey and their Wax away.
    So when a People, merely, do affect
To gather Wealth; and (foolishly secure)
Defences necessary quite neglect,
Their Foes, to spoil their Land, it will allure.
Long Peace brings War; and War brings Peace again:
For when the smart of Warfare seizeth on them,
They cry, *Alarm;* and then to fight are fain,
Until their War another Peace hath won them;
    And out of their old rusty Helmets then,
    New Bees do swarm, and fall to work again.

God, by their Names . . .

God, *by their Names, the* Stars *doth call;* *And,* hee is Ruler of *them all.*

Some say (and many men do these commend)
That all our deeds and Fortunes do depend
Upon the motions of celestial Spheres,
And on the constellations of the Stars.
If this were true, the Stars alone have been
Prime cause of all that's good, and of all sin.
And 'twere (me thinks) injustice to condemn,
Or give rewards to any, but to them.
For if they made me sin, why for that ill
Should I be damn'd, and they shine brightly still?
If they enforc'd my goodness, why should I
Be glorified for their Piety?

And if they neither good nor ill constrain,
Why then should we of Destiny complain?
   For if it be (as 'tis) absurd to say
The stars enforce us (since they still obey
Their just Commander) 'twere absurder far
To say, or think, that God's Decree it were
Which did necessitate the very same,
For which we think the stars might merit blame.
He made the stars to be an aid unto us,
Not (as is fondly dream'd) to help undo us:
(Much less, without our fault, to ruinate,
By doom of irrecoverable Fate)
And if our good Endeavours use we will,
Those glorious creatures will be helpful still
In all our honest ways: For they do stand
To help, not hinder us, in God's command;
   And he not only rules them by his pow'rs,
   But makes their Glory servant unto ours.

As soone . . .

As soone, as wee to bee, begunne ;
We did beginne, to be Vndone.

When some, in former Ages, had a meaning
An Emblem of Mortality to make,
They form'd an Infant on a Death's-head leaning,
And, round about, encircled with a Snake.
The Child so pictur'd was to signify
That from our very Birth our Dying springs;
The Snake, her Tail devouring, doth imply
The Revolution of all Earthly things.
For whatsoever hath beginning, here
Begins, immediately, to vary from
The same it was; and doth at last appear
What very few did think it should become.

The solid Stone doth moulder into Earth;
That Earth, ere long, to Water rarifies;
That Water gives an Airy Vapor birth;
And thence a Fiery-Comet doth arise:
That moves until itself it so impair
That, from a burning-Meteor, back again
It sinketh down, and thickens into Air;
That Air becomes a Cloud; then Drops of Rain;
Those Drops, descending on a Rocky-Ground,
There settle into Earth, which more and more
Doth harden still; so, running out the round,
It grows to be the Stone it was before.
    Thus, All things wheel about; and, each Beginning,
Made entrance to its own Destruction hath.
The Life of Nature ent'reth in with Sinning;
And is for ever waited on by Death:
    The Life of Grace is form'd by Death to Sin;
    And there doth Life-eternal straight begin.

This Ragge of Death . . .

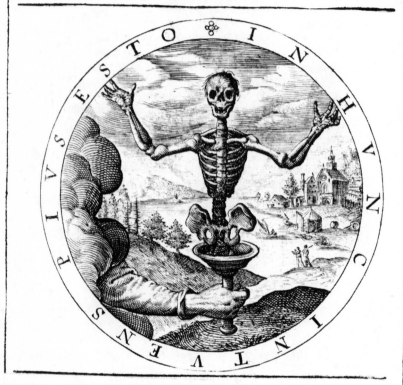

This Ragge of **Death,** *which thou shalt see,*
Consider it ; And **Pious** *bee.*

Why, silly Man! so much admirest thou
Thy present Fortune? overvaluing so
Thy Person or the beauty of thy Brow?
And Cloth'd so proudly wherefore dost thou go?
Why dost thou live in riotous Excess?
And Boast as if thy Flesh immortal were?
Why dost thou gather so? Why so oppress?
And o'er thy Fellow-creatures Domineer?
Behold this Emblem: such a thing was he
Whom this doth respresent as now thou art;
And such a Fleshless Raw-bone shalt thou be,
Though yet thou seem to act a comelier part.

Observe it well; and mark what Ugliness
Stares through the sightless Eye-holes from within:
Note those lean Crags, and with what Ghastliness
That horrid Countenance doth seem to grin.
Yea, view it well; and having seen the same,
Pluck down that Pride which puffs thy heart so high;
Of thy Proportion boast not, and (for shame)
Repent thee of thy sinful Vanity.
And having learn'd that all men must become
Such bare Anatomies; and how this Fate
No mortal Power, nor Wit, can keep thee from;
Live so, that Death may better thy estate.
Consider who created thee, and why;
Renew thy Spirit ere thy Flesh decays;
More Pious grow; Affect more Honesty;
And seek hereafter thy Creator's praise.
    So though of Breath and Beauty Time deprive thee,
    New Life, with endless Glory, God will give thee.

CHRISTOPHER HARVEY
from *The School of the Heart*

CORDIS CIRCVMCISIO.

The Circumcision of the Heart

(Circumcise the foreskin of your heart, and be no more stiffnecked. Deut. x:16.)

Heal thee? I will. But first I'll let thee know
    What it comes to.
The plaister was preparèd long ago:
    But thou must do
      Something thyself, that it may be
      Effectually apply'd to thee.

Cut out the iron sinew of thy neck,
    That it may be
Supple and pliant to obey My beck;
    And learn of Me.
      Meekness alone, and yielding, hath
      A power to appease My wrath.

Shave off thine hairy scalp, those curlèd locks
        Powd'red with pride;
Wherewith thy scornfull heart My judgements mocks,
        And thinks to hide
    Its thunder-threat'ned head, which bared
    Alone is likely to be spared.

Rip off those seeming robes, but real rags,
        Which earth admires
As honourable ornaments, and brags
        That it attires—
    Cumbers thee with indeed. Thy sores
    Fester with what the world adores.

Clip thine Ambition's wings, let down thy plumes;
        And learn to stoop
Whilst thou hast time to stand. Who still presumes
        Of strength will droop
    At last, and flag when he should fly:
    Falls hurt them most that climb most high.

Scrape off that scaly scurf of vanities
        That clogges thee so;
Profits and pleasures are those enemies
        That work thy woe:
    If thou will have Me cure thy wounds,
    First rid each humour that abounds.

The seventeenth century favored books of picture-poems with a single motif, as here the struggle between Eros and Anteros (carnal and sacred love) for the human heart. The full title of Christopher Harvey's book was: **Schola Cordis, or The Heart of it Selfe, gone away from God; brought back again to him; and instructed by him in 47 Emblems.** Published anonymously in 1647, it was for a long time falsely attributed to Francis Quarles. The emblems, by Father B. van Haeften, were engraved by William Marshall and Michel van Lechem.

CORDIS VANITAS.

The Vanity of the Heart

*(Let not him that is deceived trust in vanity; for vanity
shall be his recompence.* Job xv:31.*)*

The bane of kingdoms, world's disquieter,
Hell's heir-apparent, Satan's eldest son,
Abstract of ills, refinèd elixir,
And quintessence of sin—Ambition,
Sprung from th' infernal shades, inhabits here,
Making man's heart its horrid mansion;
 Which, though it were of vast content before,
  Is now puft up, and swells still more and more.

Whole armies of vaine thoughts it entertains;
Is stuft with dreams of kingdoms and of crowns;
Presumes of profit without care or pains;
Threatens to baffle all its foes with frowns;
In ev'ry bargain makes account of gains;
Fancies such frolic mirth as chokes and drowns
 The voice of conscience; whose loud alarms
  Cannot be heard for Pleasure's counter-charms.

See how hell's fueler his bellows plies,
Blowing the fire that burnt too fast before;
See how the furnace flames, the sparkles rise,
And spread themselves abroad still more and more;
See how the doting soul hath fixt her eyes
On her dear fooleries, and doth adore
   With hands and heart lift up, those trifling toys
   Wherewith the devil cheats her of her joys.

Alas, thou art deceiv'd; that glitt'ring crown
On which thou gazest is not gold, but grief;
That scepter, sorrow: if thou take them down,
And try them, thou shalt find what poor relief
They could afford thee, though they were thine own;
Didst thou command ev'n all the world in chief,
   Thy comforts would abate, thy cares encrease,
   And thy perplexèd thoughts disturb thy peace.

Those pearles so thorow pierc'd, and strung together,
Though jewels in thine eyes they may appear,
Will prove continu'd perils; when the weather
Is clouded once, which yet is fair and clear,
What will that fan, though of the finest feather,
Steed thee the brunt of winds and storms to bear?
   Thy flagging colours hang their drooping head,
   And the shrill trumpet's sound shall strike thee dead.

Were all those balls which thou in sport dost toss
Whole worlds, and in thy power to command,
The gain would never countervaile all the loss;
Those slipp'ry globes will glide out of thine hand;
Thou canst have no fast hold but of the Cross;
And thou wilt fall where thou dost think to stand.
   Forsake these follies, then, if thou wilt live:
   Timely repentance may thy death reprieve.

CORDIS DVRITIES

The Hardness of the Heart

(They made their hearts as an adamant stone, lest they
should heare the Lord. Zech. vii:12.)

What have we here? An heart? It looks like one;
    The shape and colour speak it such:
    But having brought it to the touch,
I find it is no better then a stone:
        Adamants are
        Softer by far.

My beams of love shine on it every day,
    Able to thaw the thickest ice,
    And where they enter, in a trice
To make congealèd crystal melt away;
        Yet warm they not
        This frozen clot.

Nay more; this hammer, that is wont to grind
    Rocks into dust and powder small,
    Makes no impression at all,
Nor dint, nor crack, nor flaw that I can find;
        But leaves it as
        Before it was.

Is Mine Almighty arme decay'd in strength?
 Or hath Mine hammer lost its weight,
 That a poor lump of earth should sleight
My mercies, and not feel My wrath at length,
  With which I make
  Ev'n heav'n to shake?

No; I am still the same, I alter not,
 And when I please, My works of wonder
 Shall bring the stoutest spirits under,
And make them to confess it is their lot
  To bow or break
  When I but speak.

But I would have men know 'tis not My Word
 Or works alone can change their hearts;
 These instruments perform their parts,
But 'tis My Spirit doth this fruit afford.
  'Tis I, not art,
  Can melt man's heart.

Yet would they leave their customary sinning,
 And so unclench the devil's claws,
 That keeps them captive in his paws,
My bounty soon should second their beginning;
  Ev'n hearts of steel
  My force should feel.

ROBERT FARLEY
from *Lychnocausia*

Whose purchase was his pouch, his house a tun,
Critic of actions whatsoever done,
That learnèd dog at noon-tide tinn'd his light,
Searching for one whose actions were upright.
The Eagle's young ones by the Sun are try'd,
Men's actions by the lamp are best espy'd;
For men in day time maskt with vizards go,
Of truth and faith making an outward show.
But when they can night's secret silence find,
Before the lamp they do unmask their mind.
Happy is he whom Sun and Lamp sees one,
Who's honest still, though witness there be none.

The Scottish poet Robert Farley's **Lychnocausia,** published
in 1638, is still another example of the Emblem book with a
single motif, in this case the delusive "outward light" of
sense compared with the divine "inner light" of spirit. That
same year Quarles also published an Emblem book on this
theme, **Hieroglyphicks of the Life of the Soul,** that far out-
shone Farley's in popularity.

Herus Lucerna.

Heros light.

Hero, who dwelt by Hellespontic strand,
Hang'd forth a Light, Leander's mark for land,
Whither his helmless course he steer'd and mov'd,
Whilst he made haste to see his well-belov'd,
Which when fierce Boreas with his blust'ring blast
Put out, he in the floods away was cast:
So that his wedding light became a torch
To convoy him to Proserpine's black porch.
   Almighty God, who made all by his power,
Holds forth his Light from the Celestial Tower:
That when the storms our tossèd souls annoy,
It may direct us to our heav'nly joy.
No storm against this Light can so prevail
But Saints unto their wisht-for Haven may sail.
Wherefor their Wedding torch this Light they have,
Which never shall convoy them to their grave.

PHILIP AYRES

from *Emblems of Love*

Ever present.

Her name is at my tongue, when ere I speak,
Her shape's before my Eyes wher ere I stir
Both day, and night, as if her Ghost did walk,
And not shee mee, but I had murdred her.

Won by Subtilty.

Life, and a Dearer Mistresse is the prize,
 For the swift Fair had ran great numbers dead.
Hippomenes ventures, bribes her covetous Eyes,
 And a gold pippin wins a Maiden head.

The poems for Ayres's book were composed by him in four
languages: Latin, English, Italian, and French. The plates, by
Otho Venius and Daniel Heinsius, were taken from a collec-
tion of Emblem poetry published in Amsterdam in 1618.

CESARE RIPA

from *Iconologia* (engravings
by Gottfried Eichler the Elder)

Dreams

The personification of **Dreams** is the spectral sleeping figure
in the foreground, half-man and half-skeleton (between life
and death), who is draped in a robe of black and white (be-
tween the night of illusion and the day of reality). In one
arm he holds a horn from which fumes arise, indicating the
vapors supposed to enter the brain and produce sleep; in the
other, he holds the caduceus of Hermes, who in his role as
Psychopompos leads mortals into the realm of sleep and
death. In the background is depicted the dream of Jacob,
during which he saw the angels of God ascending and de-
scending on a ladder connecting heaven to earth.

Ambiguity

Ambiguity is personified as a puzzled young man scratching his forehead (for youth is the age in which confusion and uncertainty most prevail) and who appears to be lost at night in a forest. He carries a lantern in his right hand (to symbolize the light of reason) and a staff in his left (to symbolize experience). The background depicts various pagan methods used to foretell the future and to resolve doubt: the Delphic oracle seated on her tripod; a priest beneath a sacred tree, blowing on a flute; a priestess holding up a human heart she has torn from a sacrificial victim; and various Oriental figures engaged in obscure rites of divination.

The World

The **World** is personified in the bearded and goat-horned god
Pan, who is dancing before a waterfall. His horns represent
the sun and moon; his flowing beard, the two masculine
"upper" elements of fire and air, which transmit their power
to the feminine "lower" elements of earth and water. The
syrinx, or "pipes of Pan," under his arm is the instrument
by which he makes all life dance to his tune. The shepherd's
crook in his other hand symbolizes dominion over nature.
He is pointing toward a labyrinth, within which can be seen
man in his four seasons, childhood, youth, maturity, and old
age, progressing toward death, who stands in the center dis-
playing a scythe and an hour-glass.

Eternity

Eternity is depicted on the stone slab in the foreground as a sirenlike bifurcated figure whose tail joins above her head to form an arch. The stars on her body represent the changeless heavens; the two balls she holds in either hand symbolize fecundity as well as fate and chance. In the background, Apollo is seen entering the cave of the god of the underworld, Demogorgon, who is writing down the laws governing the universe. Behind him sits **Eternity,** personified this time as a heavily veiled old hag, who raises her hand either in greeting or warning. The four putti on the steps represent the four ages of man; and encircling the whole scene is the serpent Uroboros, biting its tail, symbolizing the completion of another cycle of time.

JOHN BUNYAN
from *Divine Emblems*

The Frog

The Frog by nature is both damp and cold,
Her mouth is large, her belly much will hold;
She sits somewhat ascending, loves to be
Croaking in gardens, though unpleasantly.

COMPARISON

The Hypocrite is like unto this Frog;
As like as is the puppy to the dog.
He is of nature cold, his mouth is wide,
To prate, and at true goodness to deride.
And though the world is that which has his love,
He mounts his head, as if he lived above.
And, though he seeks in churches for to croak,
He neither loveth Jesus nor his yoke.

John Bunyan's **Divine Emblems: or Temporal Things Spiri-
tualized. Calculated for the use of young people,** written in
1686, two years before his death, went through numerous
popular editions under a variety of titles and with different
engravings until well into the nineteenth century.

Moses and His Wife

This Moses was a fair and comely man;
His Wife a swarthy Æthiopian:
Nor did his milk-white bosom change her skin,
She came out thence as black as she went in.

Now Moses was a type of Moses' Law,
His Wife likewise of one that never saw
Another way unto eternal life;
There's myst'ry then in Moses and his Wife.

The Law is very holy, just, and good;
And to it is espoused all flesh and blood:
But yet the Law its goodness can't bestow
On any that are wedded thereunto.

Therefore, as Moses' Wife came swarthy in,
And went out from him without change of skin;
So he that doth the Law for life adore,
Shall yet by it be left a black-a-moor.

Over-much Niceness

'Tis strange to see how over-nice are some
About their clothes, their bodies, and their home:
While what's of worth they slightly pass it by,
Not doing it at all, or slovenly.

    Their houses must well furnish'd be in print;
While their immortal soul has no good in't.
Its outside also they must beautify,
While there is in't scarce common honesty.

    Their bodies they must have trick'd up and trim:
Their inside full of filth up to the brim.
Upon their clothes there must not be a spot,
Whereas their lives are but one common blot.

    How nice, how coy are some about their diet,
That can their crying souls with hog's-meat quiet!
All must be drest t' a hair, or else 'tis naught;
While of the living bread they have no thought.
Thus for their outside they are clean and nice,
While their poor inside stinks with sin and vice.

Of the Boy and Butterfly

Behold, how eager this our little boy
Is for a butterfly, as if all joy,
All profits, honours, yea, and lasting pleasures,
Were wrapt up in her, or the richest treasures
Found in her would be bundled up together,
When all her all is lighter than a feather.

He halloos, runs, and cries out, Here, boys, here!
Nor doth he brambles or the nettles fear:
He stumbles at the mole-hills, up he gets,
And runs again, as one bereft of wits:
And all his labour and his large outcry
Is only for a silly butterfly.

JACOB CATS
from *Moral Emblems*
Smoke Is the Food of Lovers

When Cupid open'd Shop, the Trade he chose
Was just the very one you might suppose.
Love keep a shop?—his trade, Oh! quickly name!
A Dealer in tobacco—Fie for shame!
No less than true, and set aside all joke,
From oldest time he ever dealt in Smoke;
Than Smoke, no other thing he sold, or made;
Smoke all the substance of his stock in trade;
His Capital all Smoke, Smoke all his store,
'Twas nothing else; but Lovers ask no more—
And thousands enter daily at his door!
Hence it was ever, and it e'er will be
The trade most suited to his faculty:—
Fed by the vapours of their heart's desire,
No other food his Votaries require;
For, that they seek—the Favour of the Fair,
Is unsubstantial as the Smoke and air.

Like the genre paintings by his more famous countryman,
Pieter Brueghel the Elder, Jacob "Father" Cats's Emblem
poems were inspired by proverbs, folks sayings, riddles, chil-
dren's chants at play, hand-me-down mottoes, old saws, and
worn-out metaphors. Several of his poems were translated
into English by Thomas Heywood in his **Pleasant Dialogues,**
published in 1637. The court painter Sir Joshua Reynolds,
who first read Cats's Emblem books when he was introduced
to them as a child by his Dutch grandmother, remained an
enthusiastic admirer throughout his life. The selections in
this book are from **Moral Emblems,** translated by Robert
Fairlie and Joseph Pigot, and published in 1860. The engrav-
ings are by A. van de Veune, with additional illustrations by
John Leighton.

Who Cuts Off His Nose Spites His Own Face

Come here, all Friends, who know, and would
    Advise me for the best;—
I've got a Nose, the sight and thought
    Of which destroys my rest.

A Nose, alas! with wens and wheals
    Surcharged and cover'd o'er;
A huge unsightly Nose, such as
    No man e'er had before.
Oh, such a Nose! a snout so strange!
    That when I'm in the street,
Each looks at it surpris'd, and all
    The children that I meet
Point after me and say, "Oh! what
    A Nose that man has got!
Who ever saw the like of that?
    'Tis like a Porter's knot!"
At sight of it, myself, sometimes
    I'm terrified, nor know
What with it I'm to do, or if
    Yet larger it may grow.
A Nose!—but there, I've said enough;
    I cannot longer bear
So hideous a thing as this
    Upon my face to wear.
I often think I'll cut it off!—
    And why not?—why delay
To do what one hears speak of in
    The Proverb ev'ry day?
But hold! are Noses after all
    No use upon the face?
Although their shape and size be not
    Consistent quite with grace?
If cut it off I do—Why what
    An awful gap there'll be!
Without a Nose, my face will then
    Be horrible to see!
Eh! friend, put by thy knife, nor lift
    A suicidal hand
Against thyself! for as thou art,
    'Tis meet to understand,
Lies neither in thy will nor right
    To mar, nor to upbraid;
Bow meekly rather to His Will
    Who thine affliction laid!

Love, Like a Ball, Requires to Be Thrown Back

Maiden fair! if you would learn
    Well to play this pleasant game;
You must strike in quick return,
    So that I may do the same.
Should you fail to strike at all,
    And that I make play alone,
Then the shuttle's sure to fall,
    And the game at once is done.
Mark, sweet maiden, when I strike,
    And attend to what I say:
Tennis and Love's game alike
    Need a quick return of play:
Who their pleasure most would know,
    And in equal share partake,
In both games alike must show
    Equal zest to give and take.
Love and Tennis both, play'd ill,
    Soon upon the players pall,
When *one* shows a want of will
    To hit back the flying ball.
Love, to Love is demonstrative;
    Love, gives life and strength to Love,
And in being thus creative,
    Love doth most its power prove.
Love, of Love's at once the Price,
    And Reward that Love loves best;
Nothing can to Love suffice,
    But the Love that gives it rest.
If from me to Love you'd learn,
    Love; and be my Sweetheart true;
But if you give no return,
    Then I'll say—good-bye to you.

Cripple Will Always Lead the Dance

Crossing o'er a Village green,
Once I saw a pleasant scene;
Country lad   and lasses gay,
Dancing on the first of May,
Singing, shouting, full of glee;
'Twas a pleasant sight to see
How they danc'd the May-pole round,
To the Bagpipe's merry sound.
When the Piper shrillest play'd,
Greater was the noise they made;
And not one but seem'd to be
Almost mad with jollity.
But among them all was one
Who in noise the rest outdone;
He, the leader of the game,
Was both bandy-legg'd and lame,
With a club-foot of such size,
As quite fill'd me with surprise,
That so clumsy-shaped a thing
Should be leader of the ring.
So it was ne'erless, and he
First in everything would be:
Whatsoe'er was piped or sung,
Cripple's voice the loudest rung.
Nimble though young Hans might be,
Great though Claes' agility,
And though Jordan knew the way
Smartest things to Tryn to say,
Whether jump, joke, sing or bawl,
Cripple will eclipse them all.

But, as on that Village green,
Just the same is elsewhere seen:
For in Town-life much the same,
Cripple oft will lead the game:
Though to limp is all he can,
Cripple is a clever man,
And whatever may befall,
Cripple must be first of all.

Both Sides Should Be Seen

A mask, seen first in front, by children's eyes,
Strikes them with terror and with wild surprise:
But would'st restore to calm the urchin mind,
Avert the face, and let them see behind.
With men no less, how oft doth it appear,
The worst interpreter of things is Fear!
How oft the crowds of men and women grown,
Quailing like children at some form unknown!

Excess of Liberty Leads to Servitude

Until this hapless moment I was free,
And went where'er my will or fancy led;
But now oh! where—where is that liberty
So long my boast? alas! for ever fled.
Ah! woe is me that ever I was lur'd
By aught so poor and tasteless as this rind,
To enter here, before I was assur'd
Some means of exit and escape to find.

CHRISTOPHER SMART
from *Jubilate Agno*

* * *

For the letter ל which signifies GOD by himself is on the
fibre of some leaf in every Tree.

For ל is in the grain of the human heart & on the network
of the skin.

For ל is in the veins of all stones both precious and
common.

For ל is upon every hair both of man and beast.

For ל is in the grain of wood.

For ל is in the ore of all metals.

For ל is on the scales of all fish.

For ל is on the petals of all flowers.

For ל is upon all shells.

For ל is in the constituent particles of air.

For ל is on the mite of the earth.

For ל is in the water yea in every drop.

For ל is in the incomprehensible ingredients of fire.

For ל is in the stars the sun and in the Moon.

For ל is upon the Sapphire Vault.

* * *

For the AIR is purified by prayer which is made aloud
and with all our might.

For SOUND is propagated in the spirit and in all
directions.

For the VOICE of a figure is compleat in all its parts.

For a man speaks HIMSELF from the crown of his
head to the sole of his feet.

For a LION roars HIMSELF compleat from head to
tail.

For EARTH which is an intelligence hath a voice and a
propensity to speak in all her parts.

For ECHO is the soul of the voice exerting itself in
hollow places.

* * *

In his **Jubilate Agno (Rejoice in the Lamb)** Smart wrote that
his "talent is to give an impression upon words by punch-
ing, that when the reader casts his eye upon 'em, he takes
up the image from the mold. . . ." Similarly, in "On the
Name of God," Smart conceives of the Creator imposing His
holy Name on nature: El, in Hebrew the **lamed, ל**, whose
upward writhing shape, like a wisp of smoke rising from a
sacrificial altar, symbolizes the divine essence.

* * *

For the colours are spiritual.

For WHITE is the first and the best.

For there are many intermediate colours before you come to SILVER.

For the next colour is a lively GREY.

For the next colour is BLUE.

For the next is GREEN of which there are ten thousand distinct sorts.

For the next is YELLOW wch is more excellent than red, tho Newton makes red the prime.

For RED is the next working round the Orange.

For Red is of sundry sorts till it deepens to BLACK.

For black blooms and it is PURPLE.

For purple works off to BROWN which is of ten thousand acceptable shades.

For the next is PALE.

For pale works about to WHITE again.

Now that colour is spiritual appears inasmuch as the blessing of God upon all things descends in colour.

* * *

For the spiritual musick is as follows.

For there is the thunder-stop, which is the voice of God direct.

For the rest of the stops are by their rhimes.

For the Trumpet rhimes are sound bound, soar more and the like.

For the Shawm rhimes are lawn fawn moon boon and the like.

For the Harp rhimes are sing ring, string & the like.

For the Cymbal rhimes are bell well toll soul & the like.

For the Flute rhimes are tooth youth suit mute & the like.

For the Dulcimer rhimes are grace place beat heat & the like.

For the Clarinet chimes are clean seen and the like.

For the Bassoon rhimes are pass, class and the like.

For the Dulcimer are rather van fan & the like and grace place &c are of the Bassoon.

For beat heat, weep peep &c are of the Pipe.

For every word has its marrow in the English tongue for order and for delight.

WILLIAM BLAKE

from *Songs of Innocence and of Experience*

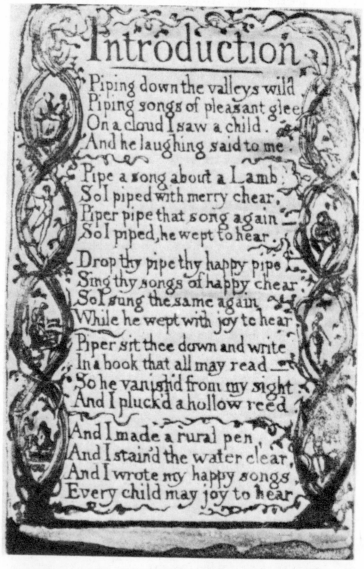

Blake's **Songs of Innocence and of Experience Shewing the Two Contrary States of the Human Soul** (1794) stems of course from the medieval tradition of the illuminated manuscript rather than from Renaissance Emblem poetry.

Infant Joy

I have no name
I am but two days old.—
What shall I call thee?
I happy am
Joy is my name.—
Sweet joy befall thee!

Pretty joy!
Sweet joy but two days old.
Sweet joy I call thee:
Thou dost smile.
I sing the while
Sweet joy befall thee.

LONDON

I wander thro' each charterd street.
Near where the charterd Thames does flow
And mark in every face I meet
Marks of weakness, marks of woe.

In every cry of every Man,
In every Infants cry of fear,
In every voice; in every ban,
The mind-forg'd manacles I hear

How the Chimney-sweepers cry
Every blackning Church appalls.
And the hapless Soldiers sigh
Runs in blood down Palace walls

But most thro' midnight streets I hear
How the youthful Harlots curse
Blasts the new born Infants tear
And blights with plagues the Marriage hearse

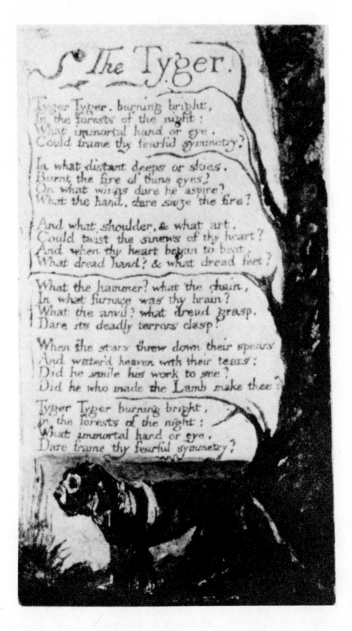

Not a very ferocious-looking tiger, hardly more than a stuffed, even a paper, tiger; but the lamb, if Blake had made it, would have had sabre teeth.

The Gates of Paradise

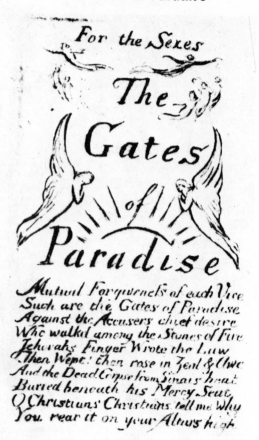

For the Sexes

The Gates of Paradise

Mutual Forgiveness of each Vice
Such are the Gates of Paradise
Against the Accusers chief desire
Who walked among the Stones of Fire
Jehovahs Finger Wrote the Law
Then Wept! then rose in Zeal & Awe
And the Dead Corpse from Sinais heat
Buried beneath his Mercy Seat
O Christians Christians tell me Why
You rear it on your Altars high

Instead of tagging Blake's epigrammatic poem at the end, as is customary, I have chosen to place the emblems with their corresponding numbered verses together and in sequence, so as to form a unified picture-poetic narrative. "Gates," the overarching symbol of the poem, stems from the theosophical writings of the German mystic Jacob Boehme, who used the expression (**Phorte,** in German) to signify the spiritual crises in life through which the soul must pass.

Blake had previously employed several of the emblems for other works (e.g., #12, depicting Ugolino and his sons in prison, for **The Marriage of Heaven & Hell;** and #13, "Death's Door," as one of his illustrations for Blair's **The Grave**). Also, Emblem #11, "Aged Ignorance," was adapted by Blake from an engraving by Otho Venius made in 1567, and entitled "Time Cutting the Wings of Cupid."

What Is Man?

The Sun's Light when he unfolds it
Depends on the Organ that beholds it.

THE KEYS

The Caterpiller on the Leaf
Reminds thee of thy Mother's Grief.

OF THE GATES

I found him beneath a Tree.

1 My Eternal Man set in Repose,
The Female from his darkness rose
And She found me beneath a Tree,
A Mandrake, & in her Veil hid me.
Serpent Reasonings us entice
Of Good & Evil, Virtue & Vice.

Water
Thou Waterest him with Tears.

2 Doubt Self Jealous, Watry folly,

Earth
He struggles into Life

3 Struggling thro' Earths Melancholy

Air
On Cloudy Doubts & Reasoning Cares

4 Naked in Air in Shame & Fear

Fire
That end in endless Strife.

5 Blind in Fire with shield & spear,
Two Horn'd Reasoning, Cloven Fiction,
In Doubt, which is Self contradiction,
A dark Hermaphrodite We stood,
Rational Truth, Root of Evil & Good.
Round me flew the Flaming Sword;
Round her snowy Whirlwinds roar'd,
Freezing her Veil, the Mundane Shell.

At length for hatching ripe he breaks the shell.

6 I rent the Veil where the Dead dwell:
When weary Man enters his Cave
He meets his Saviour in the Grave.
Some find a Female Garment there,
And some a Male, woven with care,
Lest the Sexual Garments sweet
Should grow a devouring Winding sheet.

What are these? Alas! the Female Martyr,
Is She also the Divine Image?

7 One Dies! Alas! the Living & Dead,
   One is slain & One is fled.

My Son! My Son!

8 In Vain-glory hatcht & nurst,
   By double Spectres Self Accurst,
   My Son! my Son! thou treatest me
   But as I have instructed thee.

I Want! I Want!

9 On the shadows of the Moon
   Climbing thro' Night's highest noon.

Help! Help!

10 In Time's Ocean falling drown'd.
    In Aged Ignorance profound,

Aged Ignorance.
Perceptive Organs closed, their Objects close.

11 Holy & cold, I clip'd the Wings
    Of all Sublunary Things,

Does thy God, O Priest, take such vengeance
as this?

12 And in depths of my Dungeons
    Closed the Father & the Sons.

Fear & Hope are—Vision.

13 But when once I did descry
    The Immortal Man that cannot **Die**,

*The Traveller hasteth in the
Evening.*

14 Thro' evening shades I haste away
    To close the Labours of my **Day**.

Death's Door

15 The Door of Death I open found
   And the Worm Weaving in the Ground:

I have said to the Worm:
Thou art my mother & my sister.

16 Thou'rt my Mother from the Womb,
   Wife, Sister, Daughter, to the Tomb,
   Weaving to Dreams the Sexual strife
   And weeping over the Web of Life.

To The Accuser who is
The God of This World

Truly My Satan thou art but a Dunce
And dost not know the Garment from the Man:
Every Harlot was a Virgin once
Nor canst thou ever change Kate into Nan.

Tho thou art Worshipd by the Names Divine
Of Jesus & Jehovah: thou art still
The Son of Morn in weary Nights decline
The lost Travellers Dream under the Hill

JOHN CLARE
Stone-Pit

The passing traveller with wonder sees
A deep and ancient stone-pit full of trees;
So deep and very deep the place has been,
The church might stand within and not be seen.
The passing stranger oft with wonder stops
And thinks he e'en could walk upon their tops,
And often stoops to see the busy crow,
And stands above and sees the eggs below;
And while the wild horse gives its head a toss,
The squirrel dances up and runs across.
The boy that stands and kills the black-nosed bee
Dares down as soon as magpies' nests are found,
And wonders when he climbs the highest tree
To find it reaches scarce above the ground.

Mouse's Nest

I found a ball of grass among the hay
And progged it as I passed and went away;
And when I looked I fancied something stirred,
And turned agen and hoped to catch the bird—
When out an old mouse bolted in the wheats
With all her young ones hanging at her teats;
She looked so odd and so grotesque to me,
I ran and wondered what the thing could be,
And pushed the knapweed bunches where I stood;
Then the mouse hurried from the craking brood.
The young ones squeaked, and as I went away
She found her nest again among the hay.
The water o'er the pebbles scarce could run
And broad old cesspools glittered in the sun.

The cinematic flow of Clare's imagery, with each picture
flashing by to be replaced by the next before its own after-
image has completely faded, makes these visionary sonnets
as much descriptions of Mind as of Nature.

Sunrise in Summer

The summer's morning sun creeps up the blue
O'er the flat meadows' most remotest view:
A bit at first peeps from the splendid ball,
Then more, and more, until we see it all.
And then so ruddy and so cool it lies,
The gazer views it with unwatering eyes,
And cattle opposite its kindly shine
Seem something feeding in a land divine:
Ruddy at first, yet ere a minute's told
Its burning red keeps glowing into gold,
And o'er the fenny level richly flows,
Till seeded dock in shade a giant grows;
Then blazing bright with undefinèd day
He turns the morning's earnest gaze away.

Autumn Birds

The wild duck startles like a sudden thought,
And heron slow as if it might be caught;
The flopping crows on weary wing go by,
And greybeard jackdaws, noising as they fly;
The crowds of starnels whizz and hurry by
And darken like a cloud the evening sky;
The larks like thunder rise and suther round,
Then drop and nestle in the stubble ground;
The wild swan hurries high and noises loud,
With white necks peering to the evening cloud.
The weary rooks to distant woods are gone;
With length of tail the magpie winnows on
To neighbouring tree, and leaves the distant crow,
While small birds nestle in the hedge below.

SAMUEL PALMER

Cornfield by Moonlight, with the Evening Star

from *The Sketchbook:* 1824–25

And now the trembling light
Glimmers behind the little hills, and corn,
Lingring as loth to part: yet part thou must
And though than open day far pleasing more
(Ere yet the fields and pearled cups of flowers
    Twinkle in the parting light;)
Thee night shall hide, sweet visionary gleam
That softly lookest through the rising dew:
    Till all like silver bright
    The faithful Witness, pure, and white,
Shall look o'er yonder grassy hill,
At this village, safe, and still.

All is safe, and all is still,
Save what noise the watch-dog makes
Or the shrill cock the silence breaks
    —Now and then.—
    And now and then—
    Hark!—once again,
    The wether's bell
    To us doth tell
Some little stirring in the fold.

Methinks the lingring, dying ray
Of twilight time, doth seem more fair,
And lights the soul up more than day,
When widespread, sultry sunshines are. . . .

Samuel Palmer was the most gifted of Blake's young disciples who were known as the "Shoreham Ancients": "Shoreham," because that was the small village in Kent where Palmer had a cottage and the group met on occasion; "Ancients," because they sought to renew the Gothic spirit in art and poetry. It was during the years spent in his cottage at Shoreham, when Palmer was most under the spell of Blake, that he painted his visionary landscapes, including the one at left. The accompanying poem, though written by him several years earlier, is of a piece.

EDWARD CALVERT

The Chamber Idyll

from *Visions of the Daughters of Albion*
(by William Blake)

The moment of desire! the moment of desire! The virgin
That pines for man shall awaken her womb to enormous
    joys
In the secret shadows of her chamber: the youth shut
    up from
The lustful joy shall forget to generate & create an
    amorous image
In the shadows of his curtains and in the folds of his
    silent pillow.
Are not these the places of religion, the rewards of
    continence,
The self enjoyings of self denial? why dost thou seek
    religion?
Is it because acts are not lovely that thou seekest
    solitude
Where the horrible darkness is impressed with
    reflections of desire?

Father of Jealousy, be thou accursed from the earth!
Why hast thou taught my Theotormon this accursed
     thing?
Till beauty fades from off my shoulders, darken'd and
     cast out,
A solitary shadow wailing on the margin of non-entity.

I cry: Love! Love! Love! happy happy Love! free as the
     mountain wind!
Can that be Love that drinks another as a sponge drinks
     water,
That clouds with jealousy his nights, with weeping all
     the day,
To spin a web of age around him, grey and hoary, dark,
Till his eyes sicken at the fruit that hangs before his
     sight?
Such is self-love that envies all, a creeping skeleton
With lamplike eyes watching around the frozen marriage
     bed.

But silken nets and traps of adamant will Oothoon
     spread,
And catch for thee girls of mild silver, or of furious
     gold.
I'll lie beside thee on a bank & view their wanton play
In lovely copulation, bliss on bliss, with Theotormon:
Red as the rosy morning, lustful as the first born beam,
Oothoon shall view his dear delight, nor e'er with
     jealous cloud
Come in the heaven of generous love, nor selfish
     blightings bring. . . .

Edward Calvert, like his friend Palmer, also had his inner
eye opened and the doors of perception cleansed by "The
Interpreter," as they called the aged Blake. But Calvert, who
had spent some time in Greece as a naval officer, was of a
more sensual and pagan temperament. The gemlike engrav-
ing, left , made in 1831, might have been inspired by the
passage from Blake's **Visions of the Daughters of Albion** that
accompanies it. The somewhat prudish and sanctimonious
Palmer, who owned the picture, used to keep it hidden in a
drawer in his later years.

J. W. TURNER

Slavers Throwing Overboard the Dead and Dying—
Typhon Coming On

from *The Fallacies of Hope*

Aloft all hands, strike the top-masts and belay;
Yon angry setting sun and fierce-edged clouds
Declare the Typhon's coming.
Before it strikes your decks, throw overboard
The dead and dying—ne'er heed their chains.
Hope, Hope, fallacious Hope!
Where is thy market now?

Turner's famous painting, and the accompanying poem from
his fragmentary epic narrative **The Fallacies of Hope,** com-
posed about the same time, were inspired by an event that
occurred on board the British slaveship **Zong** in 1783. After
an epidemic had broken out in the holds, the captain,
seeing that a typhoon was approaching, ordered his human
cargo thrown overboard. His motive, it seems, was to claim
the insurance for slaves who drowned, as there was none
for those who died during the voyage of illness. The story
of the atrocity, and the captain's subsequent arraignment
and trial—not for murder, of course, but for fraud—were
related in T. Clarkson's **History of the Slave Trade,** published
in 1808; but Turner may well have heard the tale in his
youth from seamen who had served on the **Zong.**

EDWARD LEAR
Nonsense Botany

Bottlephorkia Spoonifolia

Smalltoothcombia
Domestica

Tickia Orologica

Tigerlillia Terribilis

"For the right names of flowers," wrote Christopher Smart in his **Jubilate Agno,** "are yet in heaven. God make gardners better nomenclators." His prayer seems to have been heard, for not since Adam walked about in the Garden of Eden

Phattfacia Stupenda

Plumbunnia Nutritiosa

Manypeeplia Upsidownia

Guittara Pensilis

has a better nomenclator appeared on earth than Edward Lear. His mythopoeic taxonomy, in which name and image are one and inseparable, has its roots in the botanical gardens of the Mind.

Cockatooca Superba

Baccopipia Gracilis

Fishia Marina

Piggiawiggia Pyramidalis

Jinglia Tinkettlia   Nasticreechia Krorluppia

Enkoopia Chickabiddia   Barkia Howlaloudia

Extraordinary People

There was an old person of Skye,
Who waltz'd with a Bluebottle fly:
They buzz'd a sweet tune, to the light of the moon,
And entranced all the people of Skye.

There is a young lady whose nose
Continually prospers and grows;
When it grew out of sight, she exclaimed in a fright,
"Oh! Farewell to the end of my nose!"

There was an Old Lady of Chertsey,
Who made a remarkable curtsey;
She twirled 'round and round, till she sunk underground,
Which distressed all the people of Chertsey.

There was an Old Man with a beard,
Who said, "It is just as I feared!—
Two Owls and a Hen, four Larks and a Wren,
Have all built their nests in my beard!"

There was an old person of Brigg,
Who purchased no end of a wig;
So that only his nose, and the end of his toes,
Could be seen when he walked about Brigg.

There was an Old Man of Jamaica,
Who suddenly married a Quaker!
But she cried out, "O lack! I have married a black!"
Which distressed that Old Man of Jamaica.

There was a young Lady of Tyre,
Who swept the loud chords of a lyre;
At the sound of each sweep, she enraptured the deep,
And enchanted the city of Tyre.

There was an Old Man who said, "Hush!
I perceive a young bird in this bush!"
When they said, "Is it small?" he replied, "Not at all!
It is four times as big as the bush!"

LEWIS CARROLL
Mice Tails

We lived beneath the mat
Warm and snug and fat
But one woe, & that
Was the cat!
To our joys
a clog, In
our eyes a
fog, On our
hearts a log
Was the dog!
When the
cat's away,
Then
the mice
will
play,
But, alas!
one day, (So they say)
Came the dog and
cat, Hunting
for a
rat,
Crushed
the mice
all flat,
Each
one
as
he
sat
Underneath the mat, Warm & snug - Think of that!

This is the original version of Lewis Carroll's famous "mouse tail" poem as it appeared in the manuscript of **Alice's Adventures Under Ground,** later retitled and published in 1865 as **Alice's Adventures in Wonderland.** Carroll then substituted the "tail" on the page opposite, which belongs, of course, to an entirely different "mouse."

"Fury said to
a mouse, That
he met in the
house, 'Let
us both go
to law: *I*
will prose-
cute *you.*
Come, I'll
take no de-
nial; We
must have
a trial:
For really
this morn-
ing I've
nothing
to do.'
Said the
mouse to
the cur,
'Such a
trial, dear
Sir, With
no jury
or judge,
w o u l d
be wast-
ing our
breath.'
'I'll be
judge,
I'll be
jury,'
Said
cun-
ning
old
Fury:
' I ' l l
t r y
the
whole
cause,
a n d
con-
demn
you to
death.' "

Father William

I

"You are old, father William," the young man said,
    "And your hair is exceedingly white :
And yet you incessantly stand on your head—
    Do you think, at your age, it is right ?"

2.

"In my youth," father William replied to his son,
    "I feared it might injure the brain :
But now that I'm perfectly sure I have none,
    Why, I do it again and again."

In an article entitled "Alice on the Stage," published in **The Theatre** magazine in London in 1887, Carroll wrote: "I printed in manuscript, and illustrated with my own crude designs—designs that rebeled against every law of anatomy

3.

"You are old," said the youth, "as I mentioned before,
  "And have grown most uncommonly fat:
Yet you turned a back-somersault in at the door—
  Pray what is the reason of that?"

4.

"In my youth," said the sage, as he shook his gray locks,
  "I kept all my limbs very supple
By the use of this ointment, five shillings the box—
  Allow me to sell you a couple."

or art (for I had never had a lesson in drawing)——the book
which I have just had published."

Nonetheless, his own "crude designs" for **Alice in Wonderland** have a satirical bite and spontaneity that the more famous illustrations by Tenniel seem to lack.

5.

"You are old," said the youth, "and your jaws are too weak
     "For anything tougher than suet :
Yet you eat all the goose, with the bones and the beak—
     Pray, how did you manage to do it ?"

6.

"In my youth," said the old man, "I took to the law,
     And argued each case with my wife,
And the muscular strength, which it gave to my jaw,
     Has lasted the rest of my life."

7.

"You are old", said the youth, "one would hardly suppose
  "That your eye was as steady as ever:
Yet you balanced an eel on the end of your nose—
  What made you so <u>awfully</u> clever?"

8.

"I have answered three questions, and that is enough,"
  Said his father, "don't give yourself airs!
"Do you think I can listen all day to such stuff?
  Be off, or I'll kick you down stairs.!"

Stanza of Anglo-Saxon Poetry

```
ᚲWᚨS ᛒᚱYLLYᚷ, ᚦHᛑ ᛃᵉ SLYᚲHY ᚲOVES
ᛑᛁᛑ ᚷYᚱE ᚦHᛑ ᚷYHᛒLᛖ ᛁH Yᵉ WᚨᛒE:
ᚨLL HᛁHSY WEᚱE Yᵉ ᛒOᚱOᚷᚩVES;
ᚦHᛑ Yᵉ HᚩHE ᚱᚨTHS ᚩUᚲᚷᚱᚨᛒE.
```

This curious fragment reads thus in modern characters:

TWAS BRYLLYG, AND THE SLYTHY TOVES
DID GYRE AND GYMBLE IN THE WABE:
ALL MIMSY WERE THE BOROGOVES;
AND THE MOME RATHS OUTGRABE.

The meanings of the words are as follows:
BRYLLYG (derived from the verb to BRYL or BROIL). "The time of broiling dinner, i.e., the close of the afternoon."
SLYTHY (compounded of SLIMY and LITHE). "Smooth and active."
TOVE. A species of badger. They had smooth white hair, long hind legs, and short horns like a stag: lived chiefly on cheese.
GYRE, verb (derived from GYAOUR or GIAOUR, "a dog"). "To scratch like a dog."
GYMBLE (whence GIMBLET). "To screw out holes in anything."
WABE (derived from the verb to SWAB or SOAK). "The side of a hill" (from its being *soaked* by the rain).

The "Stanza of Anglo-Saxon Poetry" was inscribed in a sort of "runic" style, and then annotated with mock-turtle solemnity, by Lewis Carroll in 1855, when the author was twenty-three years old. It was part of a privately circulated collection of oddments, called **Misch-Masch**, intended for the amusement of his close friends and family. Fifteen years later it became the first stanza of the **Looking Glass** poem, "Jabberwocky." What makes this "curious fragment" even "curiouser" is the resemblance of his "runic" characters to the typescript of the phonetic alphabet invented by George Bernard Shaw.

MIMSY (whence MIMSERABLE and MISERABLE). "Unhappy."

BOROGOVE. An extinct kind of parrot. They had no wings, beaks turned up, and made their nests under sun dials: lived on veal.

MOME (hence SOLEMOME, SOLEMONE, and SOLEMN). "Grave."

RATH. A species of land turtle. Head erect: mouth like a shark: the fore legs curved out so that the animal walked on its knees: smooth green body: lived on swallows and oysters.

OUTGRABE, past tense of the verb to OUTGRIBE. (It is connected with the old verb to GRIKE or SHRIKE, from which are derived "shriek" and "creak.") "Squeaked."

Hence, the literal English of the passage is: "It was evening, and the smooth active badgers were scratching and boring holes in the hillside: all unhappy were the parrots; and the grave turtles squeaked out."

There were probably sun dials on the top of the hill, and the "borogoves" were afraid that their nests would be undermined. The hill was probably full of the nests of "raths," which ran out, squeaking with fear, on hearing the "toves" scratching outside. This is an obscure, but yet deeply affecting, relic of ancient Poetry.—ED.

Jabberwocky

'Twas brillig, and the slithy toves
　　Did gyre and gimble in the wabe:
All mimsy were the borogoves,
　　And the mome raths outgrabe.

"Beware the Jabberwock, my son!
　　The jaws that bite, the claws that catch!
Beware the Jubjub bird, and shun
　　The frumious Bandersnatch!"

He took his vorpal sword in hand:
　　Long time the manxome foe he sought—
So rested he by the Tumtum tree,
　　And stood awhile in thought.

And as in uffish thought he stood,
　　The Jabberwock, with eyes of flame,
Came whiffling through the tulgey wood,
　　And burbled as it came!

One, two! One, two! And through and through
　　The vorpal blade went snicker-snack!
He left it dead, and with its head
　　He went galumphing back.

"And hast thou slain the Jabberwock?
　　Come to my arms, my beamish boy!
O frabjous day! Callooh! Callay!"
　　He chortled in his joy.

'Twas brillig, and the slithy toves
　　Did gyre and gimble in the wabe:
All mimsy were the borogoves,
　　And the mome raths outgrabe.

"Jabberwocky" was transposed into the Shaw alphabet in 1963 by Stanley Marx and designed by Larry Alvaro, with the type by Stephen Austin and Sons, Ltd. It was first printed by Typographic Designers, New York.

ROBERT LOUIS STEVENSON
Moral Emblems

Mark, printed on this very page,
The unfortunate effects of rage.
A man (who might be you or me)
Hurls another into the sea.
Poor soul, his unreflecting act
His future joys will much contract,
And he will spoil his evening toddy
By dwelling on that mangled body.

Stevenson wrote the poems and did the woodcuts for his
Moral Emblems at Davos, Switzerland, where he was taking
a cure for TB, in 1883. They were printed by him on a toy
press that he had given to his stepson. Most likely they
were meant to parody the righteous and high-minded books

Reader, your soul upraise to see,
In yon fair cut designed by me,
The pauper by the highwayside
Vainly soliciting from pride.
Mark how the Beau with easy air
Contemns the anxious rustic's prayer,
And, casting a disdainful eye,
Goes gaily gallivanting by.
He from the poor averts his head . . .
He will regret it when he's dead.

of Emblem poetry, such as Bunyan's **Divine Emblems: Cal-
culated for the Use of Young People,** that he himself must
have been forced to endure as a child in a pious Scottish
household in Edinburgh.

The careful angler chose his nook
At morning by the lilied brook,
And all the noon his rod he plied
By that romantic riverside.
Soon as the evening hours decline
Tranquilly he'll return to dine,
And, breathing forth a pious wish,
Will cram his belly full of fish.

Industrious pirate! See him sweep
The lonely bosom of the deep,
And daily the horizon scan
From Hatteras or Matapan.
Be sure, before that pirate's old,
He will have made a pot of gold,
And will retire from all his labours
And be respected by his neighbours.
You also scan your life's horizon
For all that you can clap your eyes on.

VACHEL LINDSAY

Edgar Allan Poe

from *The Wizard in the Street*

I love him in this blatant, well-fed place.
Of all the faces, his the only face
Beautiful, tho' painted for the stage,
Lit up with song, then torn with cold, small rage,
Shames that are living, loves and hopes long dead,
Consuming pride, and hunger, real, for bread.

ROBERT DE NIRO

Verlaine at the Café Rocher

Flutter, delicate hand, beady eye—
Your angel is closer to God than you.

STÉPHANE MALLARMÉ
A Throw of the Dice Never Will Abolish Chance
(Un Coup de Dés Jamais n'Abolira le Hazard)

Just for Openers . . .

Un Coup de Dés first appeared in the international literary review **Cosmopolis** in 1897, a year before Mallarmé's death; but not until 1914, when the poem was reprinted in **La Nouvelle Revue Française,** did it receive its by now classic typographical form, in accord with his original conception. As he described it, the words and word-clusters scattered across the double-page spread would sometimes have "the look of a constellation" and at other times "seem like a vessel listing from the top of one page to the bottom of another." An attempt has been made here to reproduce this typographical form; but an exact rendering of the multifaceted idea-images of **Un Coup de Dés** into English is, of course, impossible. What has been hoped for is an approximation that, with luck, will make its point more often than it comes up craps.

Incidentally, the "diminutive shadowy form / in a siren's twisted stance" (mentioned on p. 184) may be seen depicted in Cesare Ripa's emblem for **Eternity** on p. 105.

A THROW OF DICE

NEVER

NOT EVEN WHEN WAGERED

FOR ETERNAL STAKES

FROM THE DEPTHS OF A SHIPWRECK

SO BE IT
       that

             the Abyss

white-frothed
      in slack tide
           furious
                  at an angle
                      tilts in a desperation

                       of wings

                       its own

                          in

advance tumbled back to trim its flight
                  and suppressing the spouts
                                cutting off the spray

        from far within resumes

the shadow buried in the deeps by this other sail
                        to the point of adapting
                                to the span

          its unfathomable void just like the hulk

                of a ship

            listing from one or the other side

THE MASTER

resurgent
inferring

from this conflagration

that there

as a man defies
the unique Number that can never

hesitates
a corpse by the arm
rather
than play
like a hoary lunatic
the game
for the sake of the waves
one
that shipwreck

                    beyond the age-old calculations
                    where skill is forgotten with time

                            once he gripped the helm

at his feet
                        of the unanimous horizon
prepares itself
            rouses itself and fuses
                with the fist that might grasp it
his fate and the winds

be any other
                        Spirit
                            to hurl it

                                        into the tempest
                        re-fuse division and pass proudly on

parted from the secret it keeps

invades the head
flows into the drooping beard
destined for the man
            without a spar
                    useless no
                            matter where

ancestrally not to open the hand
clenched
beyond the useless head
bequest in the devolution
to someone
ambiguous
the far-off immemorial demon
having
from realms of nothingness
induced

the old man toward this supreme conjunction with his fate

he
his childhood shadow
caressed and rubbed and combed and washed
made pliant by the waves and salvaged
from the hard bones between the planks
born
of a caprice
the sea through the old man striving or the old man against the sea
an idle chance
Betrothal

whose
fountain-sprayed veil of illusion
like the phantom of an action
will waver
will subside
madness

WILL ABOLISH

AS IF

A mere

of silence

in some nearby

flutters

insinuation

wreathed round with irony
                    or
                        the mystery
                                flung down
                                        howled out

maelstrom of horror and hilarity

about the gorge
                        without bestrewing it
                                        or escaping

                and cradles its pure meaning

                                        AS IF

bewildered solitary feather

except

for a midnight toque that meets or grazes
                    and immobilizes it
        in velvet crumpled by sardonic laughter

                    this rigid whiteness

ridiculous

                                opposed to the sky
            too much so
                        not to brand
                            however slightly
                                    whosoever

            bitter prince of the shoals

                    wears it in heroic style
                    irresistible but held
                within the brief horizon of his mind
                                as a lightning bolt

troubled
          submissive and pubescent
                                      mute

The lucid and seignorial crest
invisible on the brow
gleams
      then darkens
a diminutive shadowy form
in a siren's twisted stance

by impatient ultimate scales

laugh

    that

        IF

of vertigo

posed

  the time
    to affront
bifurcated

  a rock

  false haven
    instantaneously
      vaporized in mist

    that imposed
    a limit on the infinite

IT WAS

star-spasm

IT WOULD BE
worse

no

more no less

but inconsequentially either

THE NUMBER

WERE IT TO EXIST
other than as the far-flung hallucinations of agony

WERE IT TO BEGIN AND END
resurgent but denied and concealed when apparent
at last
by some profusion thinned to rarity

WERE IT TO BE ADDED UP

evidence of the sum if ever there was one

WERE IT TO SHINE OUT

CHANCE

There falls
the feather
rhythmic suspension of the sinister
to shroud itself
in the primal foam
where lately its delirium surged to a climax
dismayed
by the self-same indifference of the abyss

NOTHING

  of the memorable crisis
   in which
    the event

might have been accomplished for some futile
                                        human end

                WILL HAVE TAKEN PLACE
            an ordinary height pours out nothingness

                            BUT THE PLACE
    some low splashing as if to disperse the empty act
                        abruptly which otherwise
                    by its falsehood
                            might have founded
                            perdition

    in the folds
            of the wave
                    in which all being dissolves

EXCEPT
    at the zenith
          PERHAPS
              as far off as if a place

were to fuse with the beyond

                         apart from the value
                  assigned for it

                          in general

through such obliquity by such declivity

                        of fire

      towards
        it must be
          the Seven-Starred Bear with the North

                    A CONSTELLATION

        cold with oblivion and desuetude

                  but not so much
              as not to number
      on some vacant and transcendent plane
         the successive

                   sidereal shock
      of some total summing up

watching
     doubting
        rolling
          shining and meditating
             before coming to a stop
      at some final consecrated point

All Thought casts a Throw of Dice

GUILLAUME APOLLINAIRE
Woodcuts by Raoul Dufy

Orpheus

(translated by Oliver Bernard)

Marvel at this frank mastery
And these outlines' nobility:
This is the voice which the first light made heard
And for which Trismegistus found the word.

The Emblematic poems by young Apollinaire that follow
are from his first book of verse, **Le Bestiaire, ou, Cortège
d'Orphée,** published in 1911, in collaboration with Raoul
Dufy. Picasso had originally agreed to supply the emblems;
but after doing two of them (which were not used), he never
managed to complete the rest.

Tortoise

(translated by Oliver Bernard)

My certain fingers, brain of fire!
Strike the magic Thracian lyre.
The animals pass in a throng
Hearing my tortoise and my song.

"Orpheus, a native of Thrace, played a lyre given to him by
Hermes. It was formed of the shell of a tortoise . . ." (from
Apollinaire's notes to **Le Bestiaire**).

Tortoise by Raoul Dufy © 1911, S.P.A D.E.M.

Rabbit

(translated by Oliver Bernard)

There's another little cove
I'd catch living in my hand
His burrow is among the mauve
Hillocks of the Tender Land.

It's Raining
(translated by Oliver Bernard)

it is raining women's voices as if they were dead even in memory

you also are raining down marvellous encounters of my life o little drops

and these rearing clouds are beginning to whinny a whole world of auricular towns

listen to it rain while regret and disdain weep an old fashioned music

listen to the fall Of all the perpendiculars of your existence

Landscape
(translated by Anne Hyde Greet)

H
ERE   **?**
        THE   •
IS   MANSION   THIS
                                      LITTLE TREE
WHERE ARE BORN   WHICH IS BEGINNING
                                     TO BEAR FRUIT
THE   S   RE
TA   RS   SEM
AND   DIVINITIES   BLES
                                          YOU

                                                    s
                                                 e
                                              k
                                           o
                                              m
                                               s

                                          t
                                           h a t

                            R
                            E   ar
L   L   H   A LIGHTED CIG
 Y   O   T
  I   O   E
   N   G   G
      VERS   O
              T
           YOU
        SE   MY
      PA   MEM
    RA   B
   TE   E
                    R
                     S

The Stabbed Dove and the Fountain
(translated by Anne Hyde Greet)

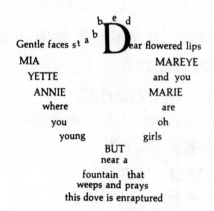

Gentle faces stabbed Dear flowered lips

MIA   MAREYE

YETTE   and you

ANNIE   MARIE

where   are

you   oh

young   girls

BUT

near a

fountain that
weeps and prays
this dove is enraptured

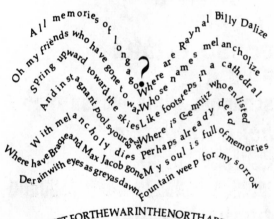

All memories of long
Oh my friends who have gone to war
Spring upward toward the skies
And in stagnant pool your eyes
With melancholy dies
Where have Braque and Max Jacob gone
De rain with eyes as grey as dawn

Where are Raynal Billy Dalize
Whose names melancholize
Like footsteps in a cathedral
Where is Cremnitz who enlisted
Perhaps already dead
My soul is full of memories
Fountain weep for my sorrow

THOSE WHO LEFT FOR THE WAR IN THE NORTH ARE FIGHTING NOW

Gardens   Evening falls O bloody sea

where   rose-laurel   warlike   flower bleeds   in abundance

HUGO BALL

KARAWANE
jolifanto bambla ô falli bambla
grossiga m'pfa habla horem
égiga goramen
higo bloiko russula huju
hollaka hollala
anlogo bung
blago bung
blago bung
bosso fataka
ä ää ü
schampa wulla wussa ólobo
hej tatta gôrem
eschige zunbada
wulubu ssubudu uluw ssubudu
tumba ba- umf
kusagauma
ba - umf

The above arty anti-art artifact by Dadaist Hugo Ball and the
one opposite by Futurist Filippo Marinetti, once the last
straw, but now as quaint as grandma's diaphragm, were
meant to explode language, and thus bring about a "Revolu-
tion of the Word" similar to the cubist revolution in art.

FILIPPO MARINETTI

JEAN (HANS) ARP
Im Autonomobilen Reich

Regierungsmitglieder

hochnehmst millionenmill um bitt
fallammelmahl fallobst toast
bum bum barind ruckturtelsack
und tabledhoten ihn vom ast

lammdi lammda im bretterbaum
im autonomobilen reich
allotria trio quartett
und hanst ihm backen in den streich

kumm kumm rindel delin ritz pfiff
bestockt beschirmt die adlerkrill
in scheiben roh gefrickt gefrackt
spiesshui derfieder schnabelschnill.

The sculptor Jean (Hans) Arp was one of the innovators
circa World War I of the method of collage dubbed **papiers
déchirés,** as in the specimen above, whereby a drawing is
torn into fragments and then pieced together to form a new
design. The poem by Arp accompanying it, in which words
have similarly been fragmented and then reformed, may also
be read as jabberwocky with a German accent.

JAMES JOYCE

Pantocracy.
Bimutualism.
Interchangeabil-
ity. Naturality.
Superfetation.
Stabimobilism.
Periodicity.
Consummation.
Interpenetrative-
ness. Predicam-
ent. Balance of
the factual by the
theoric Boox and
Coox, Amallaga-
mated.

Aun
Do
Tri
Car
Cush[1]
Shay
Shockt
Ockt
Ni
Geg[2]
Their feed begins.

MAWMAW,
LUK, YOUR
BEEEFTAY'S
FIZZIN OVER.

KAKAO-
POETIC
LIPPUDENIES
OF THE
UNGUMP-
TIOUS.

NIGHTLETTER

With our best youlldied greedings to Pep
and Memmy and the old folkers below and
beyant, wishing them all very merry Incar-
nations in this land of the livvey and plenty
of preprosperousness through their coming
new yonks

from
jake, jack and little sousoucie
(the babes that mean too)

[1] Kish is for anticheirst, and the free of my hand to him!

[2] And gags for skool and crossbuns and whopes he'll enjoyimsolff over
our drawings on the line!

This is the closing snook cocked by Joyce in **Finnegans
Wake** from the section that begins: ". . . with his broad and
hairy face, to Ireland a disgrace . . ."

EZRA POUND–JAIME DE ANGULO

je l'ai surpris
à la lisière d'un bois
à l'aurore
le lyncanthrope qui changeait sa forme

étendu dans les feuilles il dormait encore
et je vis un visage si plein de peine atroce
que je m'enfuis
épouvanté

De Angulo's Poem Translated

Werewolf in selvage I saw
In day's dawn changing his shape,

Amid leaves he lay
and in his face, sleeping, such pain
I fled agape.

The drawing of this melancholy werewolf and the poem in
French are by Jaime de Angulo. The translation is by Pound.

E. E. CUMMINGS

```
                    r-p-o-p-h-e-s-s-a-g-r
              who
   a)s w(e loo)k
   upnowgath
           PPEGORHRASS
                        eringint(o-
      aThe):l
          eA
              !p:
   S                                    a
                 (r
   rIvInG                 .gRrEaPsPhOs)
                                  to
   rea(be)rran(com)gi(e)ngly
   ,grasshopper;
```

e. e. cummings, who sought to combine the métiers of paint-
ing and poetry for "dooble delighte," first introduced the
typographical hijinks of Apollinaire into English after World
War I.

un
der fog
's
touch

slo

ings
fin
gering
s

wli

whichs
turn
in
to whos

est

people
be
come
un

l(a

le
af
fa

ll

s)
one
l

iness

KENNETH BURKE
Flowerishes

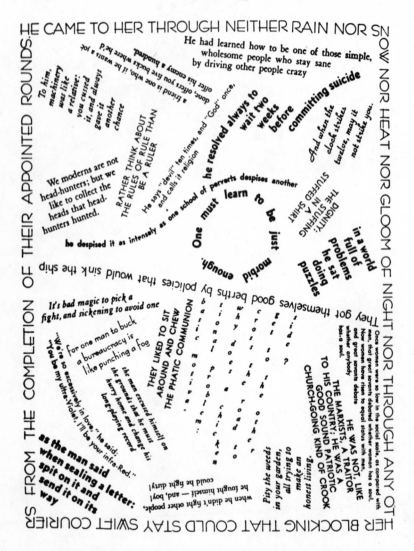

Kenneth Burke's boxed-in improvisations might be described as formalized graffiti: a contradiction in terms, no doubt, yet somehow befitting the author of **Perspectives by Incongruity** and **Rules for Disorder**.

BOB BROWN

*I preen
My quills*

*I always preen my
Pen quills
Like a peacock*

Before I start to

goose-step with them

WITH A SHAKE +
WITH A SHIVER
I SHED THE LEAVES
MY POET-TREE

These indelibly Yankee, yet somehow Pompeian, doodles by the late expatriate poet and bon vivant Bob Brown were set down by him with his Magic Marker sometime during the American heyday twenties in Paris.

CUPIDS
HAVE MADE PUBLIC
TOO LONG
THEIR PRIVATE PARTS

THEY HAVE THRUST
THEIR DIMPLED DELIGHTS
TOO PUBLICLY INTO
MY PRIVATE FACE

VIGNETTE

PINK CHEEKS

WOMEN, READING + WEEPING
LONG TEAR TRICKLES
DOWN PALE
MADONNA CHEEKS
ADOWN ARISTOCRATIC
BLUE NOSES
O RABELAIS
SLAP FOR ME
THEIR FLABBY FAT
PINK CHEEKS

CHARLES HENRI FORD
Spare Parts

The technique of **papiers (or mots) déchirés** has here been imported into American Pop art by the surrealist poet Charles Henri Ford.

LIVING WITH _The incredible_ palm-sized Columbus

[Father's Day is June 21st]

Doesn't someone wash-and-wear *out*   Who's drinking all that

— **air**   Here he comes
          ...ready or not!   IS HE OR AIN'T HE

Magnificent   **It's** the beautiful mouth...

STYLED BY ANDREAS FOR C.H.   just one of the many   *The*
          search is naked and **all** messy ...then

It gently plumps itself up!   **WHO TRIED** the
          mould

Sure Glad you **make** it FIT   today's

friskier **jury of** "extras" are
          LIP⊙LOX ...**AND** like you watch

THIS YEAR they would rather **pay** a cargo of misused ladies *let them!*

These boots trip on comforts down below   **SEE IT ALL** is at it

HE may catch up with A HY-LO **do** KIT FIRST CLASS bagful of ▄▄
          ▄▄
          ▄▄
          ▄▄
          will!   Boy,

what a difference ...whatever you do **every** SOMETHING KEENS YOU —**it's no place** TO **shed**

Go ahead **rooster** WITH new style of game   **ZZOOOMMM**

people take you home
and love you!

The motto for
the new age is: *little repairs* **soften it**

KENNETH PATCHEN
His Suchamuch?

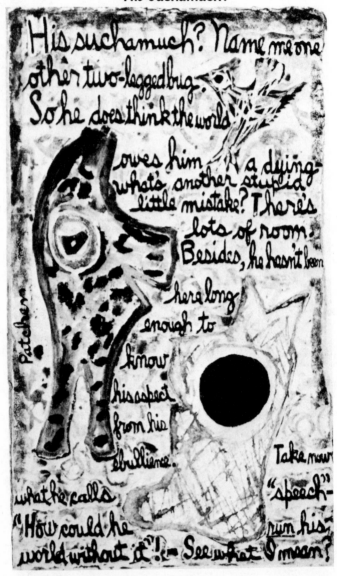

The poems **cum** pictures by Kenneth Patchen, and those by Stevie Smith and Russell Edson that follow, are not "illustrated" poetry, but rather the poems themselves extended into the modality of the visible.

It's Outside

The Man Who Was Shorter Than Himself

There was a man two inches shorter than himself
Who always kept getting stuck in the sidewalk;
And when the curious townsmen came
To yank his arms and crush his hat,
He'd spit in the eye of the lean,
And steal the wallets off the fat.

The Murder of Two Men by a Young Kid Wearing Lemon-Colored Gloves

Wait.

Wait.

Wait.

Wait. Wait.

Wait.

Wait.

W a i t .

Wait.

Wait.

Wait.

Wait.

Wait.

Wait.

NOW.

STEVIE SMITH

Lady "Rogue" Singleton

Come, wed me, Lady Singleton,
And we will have a baby soon
And we will live in Edmonton
Where all the friendly people run.

I could never make you happy darling,
Or give you the baby you want,
I would always very much rather, dear,
Live in a tent.

I am not a cold woman, Henry,
But I do not feel for you,
What I feel for the elephants and the miasmas
And the general view.

The Face

There is a face I know too well,
A face I dread to see,
So vain it is, so eloquent
Of all futility.

It is a human face that hides
A monkey soul within,
That bangs about, that beats a gong,
That makes a horrid din.

Sometimes the monkey soul will sprawl
Athwart the human eyes,
And peering forth, will flesh its pads,
And utter social lies.

So wretched is this face, so vain,
So empty and forlorn,
You well may say that better far
This face had not been born.

Chaps

Private Means is dead
God rest his soul, officers and fellow-rankers said.

Captive Good, attending Captain Ill
Can tell us quite a lot about the Captain, if he will.

Major Portion
Is a disingenuous person
And as for Major Operation well I guess
We all know what his reputation is.

The crux and Colonel
Of the whole matter
(As you may read in the Journal
If it's not tattered)

Lies in the Generals Collapse Debility Panic and Uproar
Who are too old in any case to go to the War.

Not Waving But Drowning

Nobody heard him, the dead man,
But still he lay moaning:
I was much further out than you thought
And not waving but drowning.

Poor chap, he always loved larking
And now he's dead
It must have been too cold for him his heart
They said.   [gave way,

Oh, no no no, it was too cold always
(Still the dead one lay moaning)
I was much too far out all my life
And not waving but drowning.

RUSSELL EDSON

A Stone Is Nobody's

A man ambushed a stone. Caught it. Made it a prisoner. Put it in a dark room and stood guard over it for the rest of his life.

His mother asked why.

He said, because it's held captive, because it is the captured.

Look, the stone is asleep, she said, it does not know whether it's in a garden or not. Eternity and the stone are mother and daughter; it is you who are getting old. The stone is only sleeping.

But I caught it, mother, it is mine by conquest, he said.

A stone is nobody's, not even its own. It is you who are conquered; you are minding the prisoner, which is yourself, because you are afraid to go out, she said.

Yes yes, I am afraid, because you have never loved me, he said.

Which is true, because you have always been to me as the stone is to you, she said.

Movements

In the wheel is the round shape.

The road is calling only that it is open; and you flow naturally into it, closing something behind you as you enter out of the foreground.

You fall from a door, you fall down a road. You can get nothing, can hold nothing; your finger bones fall away like cigarette butts.

But in the wheel, forever, see it, the shape moving through its own channel like a stillness.

You are falling through your whole life. You are breaking apart. But, in the wheel is something even more than the shape of the wheel, the idea which is the bone upon which the flesh of the wheel is fixed.

Waiting for the Signal Man

A woman said to her mother, where is my daughter?

Her mother said, up you and through me and out of grandmother; coming all the way down through all women like a railway train, trailing her brunette hair, which streams back grey into white; waiting for the signal man to raise his light so she can come through.

What she waiting for? said the woman.

For the signal man to raise his light, so she can see to come through.

An Animal, or What Happened in a Wood

A large animal killed an old man in the wood one day. The animal put on the old man's clothes. The animal did not know how to tie the laces on an old man's shoes. It did not matter. Nothing matters now. The animal put one of the old man's shoes on its head, and his hat on one of its feet. But, that as it walked grew weary of having its foot in the hat, and with rage kicked it away.

The hat landed on a turtle. The turtle found itself isolated and in darkness, surrounded by human odor. At first it felt that the hat must be a human stomach, and that it was swallowed. But seeing that it was not dead nor in pain, and that it could move even with this human burden, it continued. And so a man's hat was seen moving slowly in a wood.

The animal came to a house. An old woman came out and started to beat the animal, screaming, where is your father?

MAY SWENSON
How Everything Happens
(Based on a Study of the Wave)

```
                                            happen.
                                      to
                                   up
                              stacking
                           is
                 something
When nothing is happening


When it happens
              something
                        pulls
                             back
                                not
                                  to
                                    happen.



When                                    has happened.
     pulling back        stacking up
                happens


         has happened                               stacks up.
When it               something                nothing
                           pulls back while




Then nothing is happening.



                                  happens.
                               and
                        forward
                     pushes
                   up
              stacks
        something
Then
```

Stone Gullets

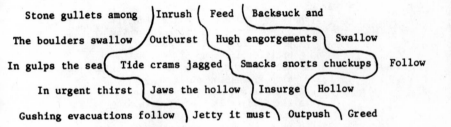

```
Stone gullets among    Inrush   Feed   Backsuck and
The boulders swallow   Outburst   Hugh engorgements   Swallow
In gulps the sea   Tide crams jagged   Smacks snorts chuckups   Follow
In urgent thirst   Jaws the hollow   Insurge   Hollow
Gushing evacuations follow   Jetty it must   Outpush   Greed
```

JOHN HOLLANDER
Swan and Shadow

```
                      Dusk
                   Above the
               water hang the
                       loud
                       flies
                      Here
                      O so
                      gray
                      then
                      What              A pale signal will appear
                      When           Soon before its shadow fades
                      Where         Here in this pool of opened eye
                      In us     No Upon us As at the very edges
                    of where we take shape in the dark air
                     this object bares its image awakening
                       ripples of recognition that will
                        brush darkness up into light
      even after this bird this hour both drift by atop the perfect sad instant now
                         already passing out of sight
                       toward yet-untroubled reflection
                      this image bears its object darkening
                    into memorial shades Scattered bits of
                    light    No of water Or something across
                    water        Breaking up No Being regathered
                    soon         Yet by then a swan will have
                    gone            Yes out of mind into what
                    vast
                    pale
                    hush
                    of a
                    place
                    past
              sudden dark as
                 if a swan
                    sang
```

Eskimo Pie

```
         I shall
      never pretend
    to have forgotten
    such loves as those
    that turned the dying
    brightness at an end of
    a childs afternoon into
    preludes To an evening of
    lamplight To a night dark
    with blanketing To mornings
    of more and more There deep
    in the old ruralities of play
    the frosted block with papery
    whisps still stuck to it kissed
    me burningly as it arose out of
    dry icy stillnesses And there now
    again I taste first its hard then
    its soft Now I am into the creamy
    treasure which to have tasted is to
    have begun to lose to the heat of a
    famished sun But O if I break faith
    with you poor dreadful popsicle may
    my mouth forget warm rains a tongue
    musty Pauillac cool skin all tastes
                    I see
                    sweet
                    drops
                    slide
                    along
                    a hot
                    stick
                    It is
                    a sad
                    sorry
                    taste
                    which
                    never
                    comes
                    to an
                    end
```

CHRISTOPHER MIDDLETON
Homage to Kafka

```
cage cage     cage cage     cage cage     cage cage
cage cage     cage cage     i    cage     cage    b
cage cage     cage cage     cage cage     cage cage

cage    r     cage cage     cage   ir     cage cage
cage cage     cage cage     cage cage     cage cage
cage cage     d    cage     d    cage     cage cage

cage    r     cage   bi     cage cage     cage cage
cage cage     cage    d     rd   cage     cage cage
i    cage     cage cage     b    cage     cage    b

cage cage     d    cage     cage   b      cage cage
cage cage     cage cage     cage   b      cage cage
cage cage     d    cage     r    cage     cage cage

cage cage     cage   i      cage cage     cage cage
cage cage     cage cage     cage cage     cage cage
cage cage     cage cage     cage cage     cage cage

b    cage     b    cage     r    cage     cage cage
cage   rd     cage cage     cage cage     cage cage
bi   cage     cage   bi     cage cage     cage cage

r    cage     id   cage     cage   bi     bird bird
cage cage     cage   ir     rd   bird     bird bird
cage   bd     i    cage     bird bird     bird bird
```

EDWIN MORGAN

```
                    pomander
                 open pomander
               open poem and her
               open poem and him
              open poem and hymn
             hymn and hymen leander
             high man pen meander
            o pen poem me and her
            pen me poem me and him
              om mane padme hum
             pad me home panda hand
            open up o holy panhandler
          ample panda pen or bamboo pond
         ponder a bonny poem pomander opener
       open banned peon penman hum and banter
      open hymn and pompom band and panda hamper
       o i am a pen open man or happener
          i am open manner happener
             happy are we open
                poem and a pom
               poem and a panda
               poem and aplomb
```

```
a not only is
  my flight true
     but my piercing strong My point is buried but not lost Asleep not
  dead it dreams
n a straw bed
```

THOMAS MERTON

W H I S K E

W H I S K

W H I S S S

K E E Y

S H K E E Y

W H I S K W

H I S K W Y

W H I S K Y

whisk E Y

EYE hisky

W H I S K W

aaaa s h ky

w h I S key

YK e h w ik

W H I S K I

h s e y k w

H I s k e y

W I S H K I

DICK HIGGINS

```
       assass
        ss
         ass
         ass
         ss
        sss
        sss
     glasss
       ass
       assglass
         ss

       sslass
       ss
       ssglass
     lassass
       ssglass
       asslass
       sss
       ssglass
       ssass
       sslass
       ss
     lassss
          glass
     asslass
       sslass
     assss
         slass
       ssass
     assss
     assass
       sslass
     asss
          glass
```

SIMON CUTTS

sky
so
thin

LYS

IRIS

LƧY

IRYS

LƧYS

ISꞄS

skin
so
soft

sky
so
thin

featherware
fairweather

apple ladder
windfall trolley

The Dutch Fruit Economy

clogs
windmill cogs
apple logs
apples

Family

Lily is in
the water.
Iris is not

cloudsheep cloudsheep cloudsheep   cloudsheep
cloudsheep cloudsheepcloudsheep cloudsheep

clouds heep   clouds heep clouds clouds
clouds clouds heep clouds heep clouds

MILTON KLONSKY

Two in the Bush

clenching, un-
clenching, an

an-
gry grisgris or

grim
Stymphalian

bird-fist
swept past and just missed.

Palimpsest

Time with his old face
Death with his skull face
God with his No Face
Under my own face

. . . like walking into oneself in a mirror.

Chinoiserie

人

poor bare forked

人 人
jen–jen
man–man

m
a
n

f r o m

u m

p

J

l
i
k
e

a

l l
i
a
f   s h
l
e
a

The Bogie Man Cometh

With his lumpy sack
Hu
   m
      ped upon his back;
And his schnorer's coat and raucous cries
And compass-needle nervous eyes;
And his moon-weird shadow that can throw
Its own shadowier shadow;
And his orc's arms stretched out out of shapes of
Nightmares of narrow escapes;
And his forlorn last long high hard squawk
Pitched up from the courtyard:
Aiiiiiieee biiiiiieeeee ohwillllld clohoooooooze!
And the red wart on his nose;
And a wide smile on his awry face
Like a baby's rump turned sideways.

The drawing is by Lyndia Utter, eleven years old, a student
at Ms. Janet Fish's art class in Carnegie Hall.

EUGEN GOMRINGER
(translated by Jerome Rothenberg)

words are shadows
shadows become words

words are games
games become words

are shadows words
do words become games

are games words
do words become shadows

are words shadows
do games become words

are words games
do shadows become words

The daedalian Swiss poet-painter Eugen Gomringer describes his poetic credo as follows: "The constellation, the word-group, replaces the verse: instead of syntax it is sufficient to allow two, three, or more words to achieve their full effect. . . . In finding, selecting and putting down these words (the poet) creates 'thought-objects' and leaves the task of association to the reader, who becomes a collaborator and, in a sense, the completer of the poem."

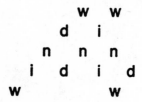

the black mystery
is   here
here   is
the black mystery

Roads 68

(translated by Jerome Rothenberg)

SHELL and
ESSO

ESSO and
TEXACO

TEXACO and
BP

BP and
TEXACO

TEXACO and
SHELL

SHELL and
BP

BP and
ESSO

ESSO and
SHELL

SHELL and
TEXACO

TEXACO and
ESSO

ESSO and
BP

BP and
SHELL

the common
smell

```
                            IVIV
                          IVIVIV
                        IVIVIVIV
                  IVIV  IVIV
                IVIV    IVIV
              IVIV      IVIV
            IVIV        IVIV
          IVIV          IVIV
        IVIV            IVIV
      IVIV              IVIV
    IVIV                IVIV
  IVIV                  IVIV
IVIV IVIV IVIV IVIV IVIVIVIVIVIV IVIV
IVIV IVIV IVIV IVIV IVIVIVIVIVIV IVIV
                        IVIV
                        IVIV
                        IVIV
                        IVIV
                        IVIV
                        IVIV
                        IVIV
                        IVIV
```

```
4444 4444                                                    4444
4444  4444                                                  4444
4444   4444                                                4444
4444    4444                                              4444
4444     4444                                            4444
4444      4444                                          4444
4444       4444                                        4444
4444        4444                                      4444
4444         4444                                    4444
4444          4444                                  4444
4444           4444                                4444
4444            4444                              4444
4444             4444                            4444
4444              4444                          4444
4444               4444                        4444
4444                4444                      4444
4444                 4444                    4444
4444                  4444                  4444
4444                   4444                4444
4444                    4444            4444
4444                     44444444
4444                      444444
4444                       4444
```

schif schif schif schif schif schif
fihcs fihcs fihcs fihcs fihcs
hcsif hcsif hcsif hcsif hcsif
fisch fisch fisch fisch fisch
hcsif hcsif hcsif hcsif hcsif hcsif
fisch fisch fisch fisch fisch fisch
hcsif hcsif hcsif hcsif hcsif hcsif
fisch fisch fisch fisch fisch fisch
schif schif schif schif schif schif
fihcs fihcs fihcs fihcs fihcs fihcs

fisch = fish
schif(f) = boat

IAN HAMILTON FINLAY

The most prolific as well as influential exponent of Concrete poetry in England, Finlay has extended its range into sculpture, ceramics, compositions on glass, sun dials, models of sailing ships, horticulture, posters and postcards, and other media.

m
Mm
x
m
m Mm
x
m
mm
m
mm
x
MmM
mm
m
m
mm
m
x
mmm
m
m
mm
x
m
mmMm
m
x
m
mm
m
this
is
the
little
burn
that
plays
its
mm
mMm
m
mmouth-
organ
by
the
m
mm
mmm
mMm
mill
x
mm
Mmm

"The 'XM poem' is less concrete than 'fauve.' A little burn (stream) flows with a sound which suggests tunes on a mouth organ. Its path is denoted by the x's and m's, the m's being the sound and the x's a wind-mill, as well as the conventional sign for kisses—of light on water, perhaps—and signs of happiness. Different sizes and kinds of type suggest the altering nature of the water." (I.H.F.)

```
        pair g.
      rl au pair
     ɔair girl au
     au pair girl
    ʃu pair girl a.
   ʃrl au pair girl ɑ
  ɔair girl au pair gir.
 ɡirl au pair girl au pair
 ɔair girl au pair girl au pɑ
air girl au pair girl au pair
pair girl au pair girl au pa
ʃu pair girl au pair girl aɪ
  ʃirl au pair girl au pair
   ɔirl au pair girl ⌐
```

Homage to Seurat

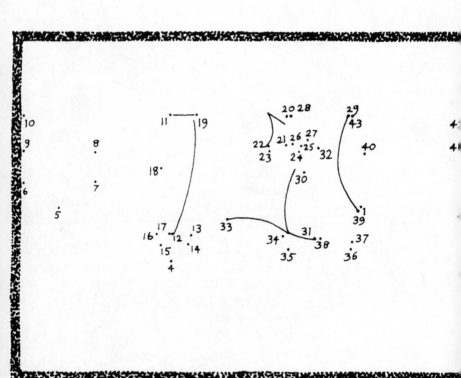

a peach
an apple

a table

an eatable
peach

an apple

an eatable
table
apple

an apple
a peach

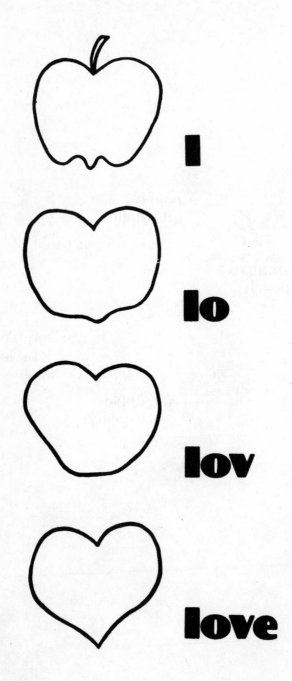

a   a   a   a   a
   c   c   c   c
r   r   r   r   r
   o   o   o   o
b   b   b   b   b
   a   a   a   a
t   t   t   t   t
   s   s   s   s
t   t   t   t   t
   a   a   a   a
b   b   b   b   b
   o   o   o
r   r   r   r   r
   c   c   c   c
a   a   a   a   a

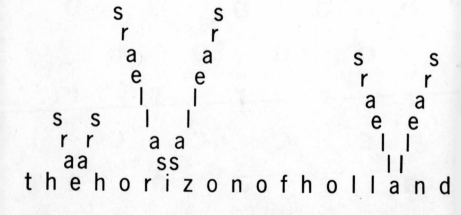

PAUL DE VREE

Eeroo

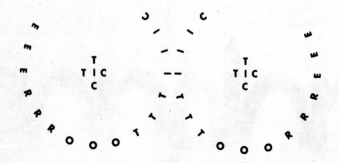

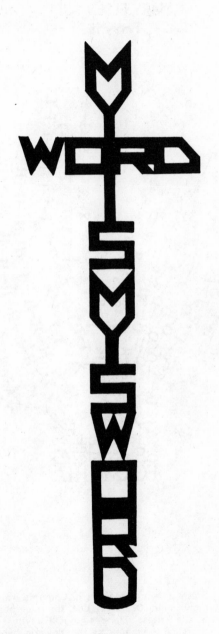

MARY ELLEN SOLT
Forsythia

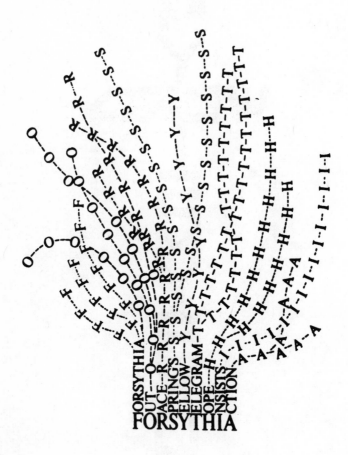

Mary Ellen Solt's perennial **Flowers in Concrete** were set by the typographer John Dearstyne. Of the one above, the most famous, she writes: "The design of 'Forsythia' is made from the letters of the name of the flowering shrub and their equivalents in the Morse Code. The text is part of the design."

Wild Crab

Wind, Intrudes, Lifting Day,
Cantabile, cantabile

Lilac

SALETTE TAVARES

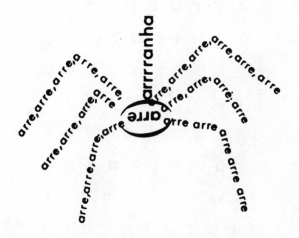

aranha = spider
arre = cry (like *gee up!*) used to make donkeys go
    faster; also, a swear word or ejaculation of anger
arrranha = *aranha* (spider) + *arranha* (scratch)
arrranhisso = *aranha* + *arranha* + *isso* (that)
arranhaço = *aranha* + *aço* (steel); therefore, a hard,
    deep scratch

Concrete poetry may be said to have found "a local habita-
tion and a name" in São Paulo, Brazil, for it was there that
the movement was first conceived as such by the poets of
the so-called "Noigandres" group, centered around the mag-
azine **Invençao,** during the early 1950s.

AUGUSTO DE CAMPOS
Caracol

colocar a m a s
caracolo c a r
a m a s **caracol**
o c a r a m a s **car**
acolo c a r a m a
s **caracol**o c a
r a m a s **caraco**
lo c a r a m a s **ca**
racolo c a r a m
a s **caracol**o c
a r a m a s **carac**
o lo c a r a m a s **c**
aracolo c a r a
m a s **caracol**o
c a r a m a s **cara**

colocar a mascara = to put on the mask
mascara = mask, (it) masks
mas = but
cara = face
caracol = snail

The snail **(caracol)** within this carapace of "masked" words peeps out from time to time, and from line to line, as it crawls slowly down the page.

RONALDO AZEREDO

r u a r u a r u a s o l

r u a r u a s o l r u a

r u a s o l r u a r u a

s o l r u a r u a r u a

r u a r u a r u a s

sol = sun
rua = street

One can see the **sol** gradually setting down the poem, projecting the long vertical shadow of the midday "l," until it finally disappears beyond the **rua** in the West.

PEDRO XISTO
Epithalamium—II

S = serpent
h = he (Adam)
e = Eve

Wind-Leaf

```
wind   wind   wind   wind   wind
  wind   leaf   wind   leaf   wind
leaf   wind   leaf   wind   leaf
  wind   leaf   wind   leaf   wind
leaf   wind   leaf   wind   leaf
  wind   leaf   wind   leaf   wind
leaf   wind   leaf   wind   leaf
  leaf   leaf   leaf   leaf   leaf
```

FLORIVALDO MENEZES
Reverence

The Portuguese title for this sequence is **R ever Excia,** combining the senses of "Your Excellency" and "Reverence." It is based on the logotype for RÉUNOS, an automotive company in Brazil.

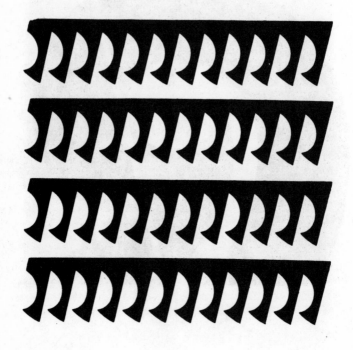

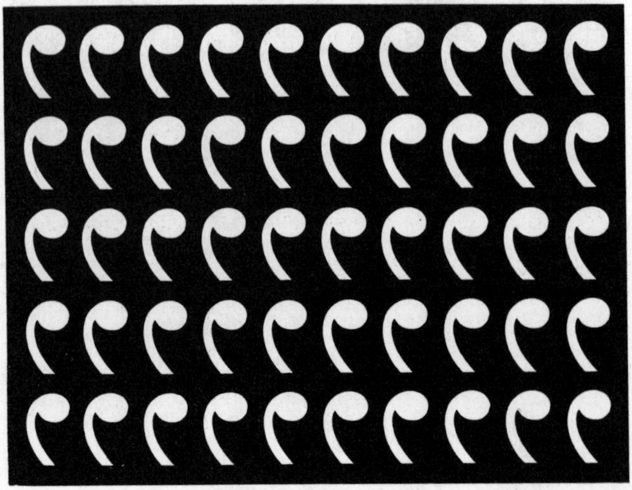

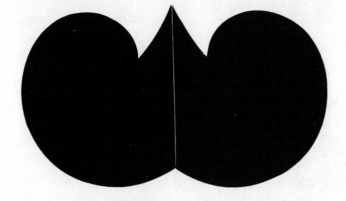

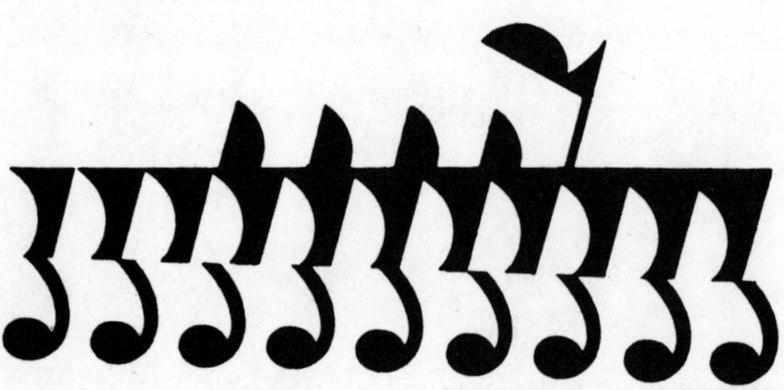

SEIICHI NIIKUNI

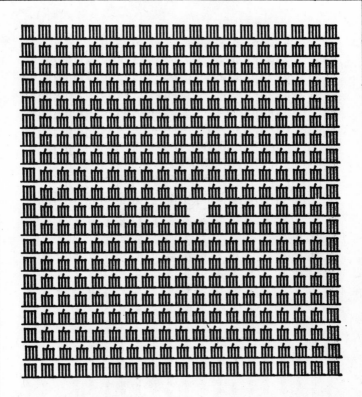

Ⅲ = dish

血 = blood

In the following picture-poems from Japan, the rare and ancient art of calligraphy seems to have been presto-changoed into typography. What Ezra Pound once imagined Oriental characters to be—abstract ideas directly represented by pictograms—has at last been made concrete, or, as the saying goes, "They speak for themselves."

Darkness

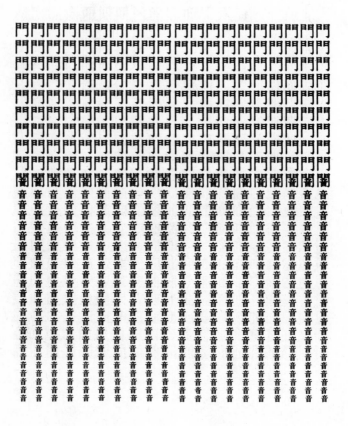

門 = door
闇 = obscurity
音 = sound

川川川川川川川川川川川川川川川川川川川川川川川
川川川川川川川川川川川川川川川川川川川川川川州
川川川川川川川川川川川川川川川川川川川川川州州
川川川川川川川川川川川川川川川川川川川川州州州
川川川川川川川川川川川川川川川川川川川州州州州
川川川川川川川川川川川川川川川川川州州州州州州
川川川川川川川川川川川川川川川川州州州州州州州
川川川川川川川川川川川川川川川州州州州州州州州
川川川川川川川川川川川川川川州州州州州州州州州
川川川川川川川川川川川川川州州州州州州州州州州
川川川川川川川川川川川川州州州州州州州州州州州
川川川川川川川川川川川州州州州州州州州州州州州
川川川川川川川川川川州州州州州州州州州州州州州
川川川川川川川川川州州州州州州州州州州州州州州
川川川川川川川川州州州州州州州州州州州州州州州
川川川川川川川州州州州州州州州州州州州州州州州
川川川川川川州州州州州州州州州州州州州州州州州
川川川川川州州州州州州州州州州州州州州州州州州
川川州州州州州州州州州州州州州州州州州州州州州
州州州州州州州州州州州州州州州州州州州州州州州

川 = river
州 = sandbank

A River Has Already Been Reduced to Skin

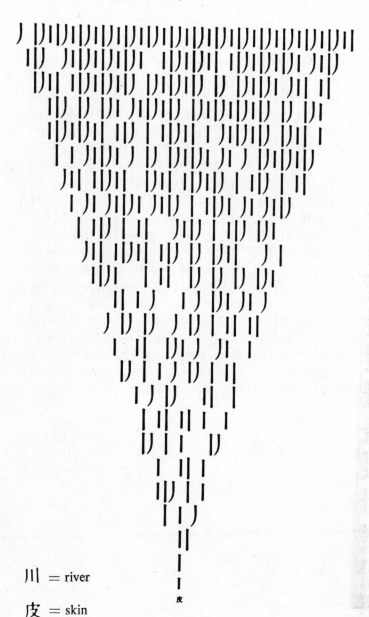

川 = river

皮 = skin

SHOJI YOSHIZAWA
An Image

影 = shadow

FUMIO KAMIIE

午 = noon

芊 = sweat

CHIMA SUNADA
Loneliness Doesn't Betray

独 = loneliness
楽 = pleasure
独楽 = top

Living and Death

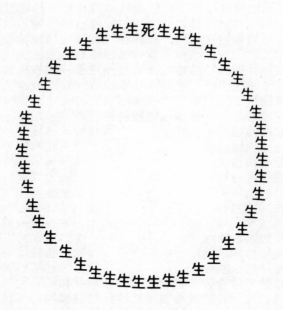

生 = living

死 = death

HIRO KAMIMURA
Water and Ice

水 = water

氷 = ice

JOCHEN GERZ
The Tree of the Silent Majority

REINHARD DÖHL
Worm in Apple

ApfelApfelApfelApfel
pfelApfelApfelApfelApfelA
felApfelApfelApfelApfelApfe
ApfelApfelApfelApfelApfelApf
pfelApfelApfelApfelApfelApfel
ApfelApfelApfelApfelApfelApfe
pfelApfelApfelApfelApfelApfelA
ApfelApfelApfelApfelApfelApfe
felApfelApfelApfelApfelApfel
pfelApfelApfelApfelApfelApf
elApfelApfelApfelWurmAp
elApfelApfelApfelApfel
pfelApfelApfelApfel
pfelApfelApfelA
pfelApfel

CLAUS BREMER

```
is the text the text left out
is the tex  he text left out
 is the te   e text left out
  is the t     text left out
   is the      text left out
   is the      ext left out
    is th      xt left out
    is t        t left out
     is           left out
     is           left out
      i           eft out
                  ft out
      t            t out
     th             out
     the            out
     the             ut
     the t            t
     the te
     the tex          t
     the text        xt
     the text        ext
     the text l      text
     the text le      text
     the text lef    e text
     the text left   he text
     the text left   the text
     the text left e    the text
     the text left ou  s the text
     the text left out is the text
```

HANSJÖRG MAYER
Alphabet 1962, Typoem "A" and "Z"

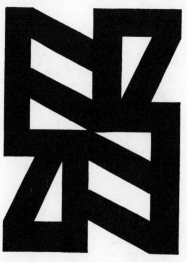

TOM OCKERSE
Cloud/Horizon/Water

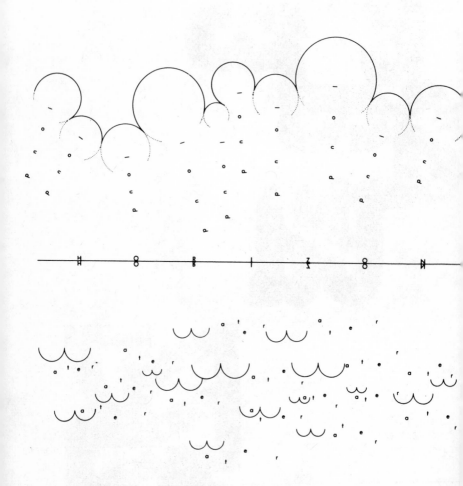

Velocity

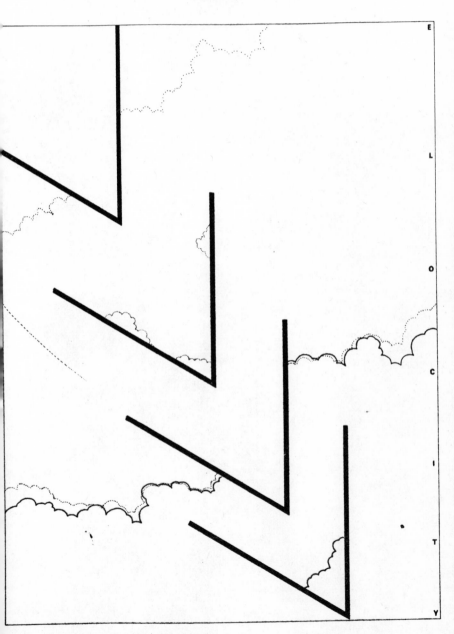

DiVision

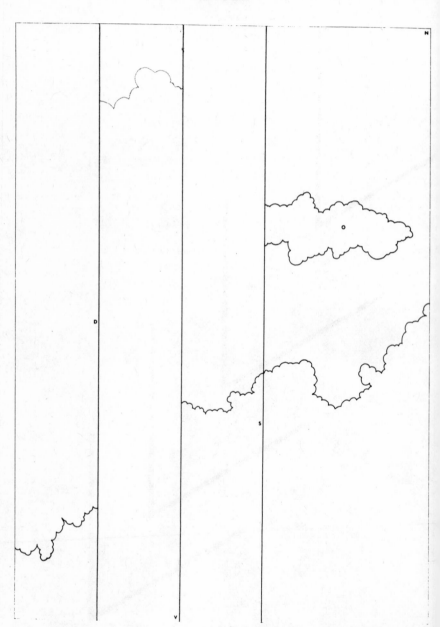

Dimension

N   S

D   I

          N

          O   I

E   M

JONATHAN WILLIAMS
Five Jargonelles from the Herbalist's Notebook

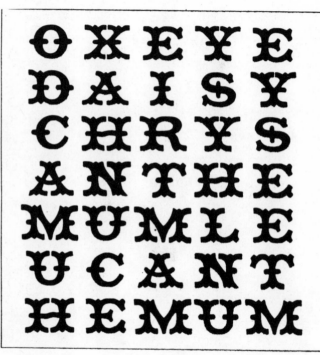

A Blazon, Built of the Commonest of All
Common Eurasian Weeds of the Fields
and the Wayside

The typographical designs for these native woodnotes are by
Dana Atchley.

```
WAHUHU WAHUHU WAH
UKU UGUKU UGUKU UGU
U HUHU HUHU HUHU HU
LALU LALU LALU LA
TU TALATU TALATU TAL
TSIKILILI TSIKILILI
IKIKI TSIKIKI TSIKIKI T
U KAGU KAGU KAGU KA
YA WAYA WAYA WAYA
YEAH YEAH YEAH YEAH
NA GUNA GUNA GUNA GU
SA SASA SASA SASA S
UNU KUNUNU KUNUNU
DUSTU DUSTU DUSTU D
```

A Chorale* of Cherokee Night Music As
Heard Through an Open Window in
Summer Long Ago

---

* screech owl/hoot owl/yellow-breasted chat/jar-fly/cricket/Caro-
lina chickadee/Katydid/crow/wolf/beetle/turkey/goose/bullfrog/
spring frog

3 Ripples in the Tuckasegee River

KUK

KUK KUK

KUK·KUK

KUKKUK

A PILEATED WOODPECKER'S RESPONSE TO
FOUR DOGWOOD BERRIES

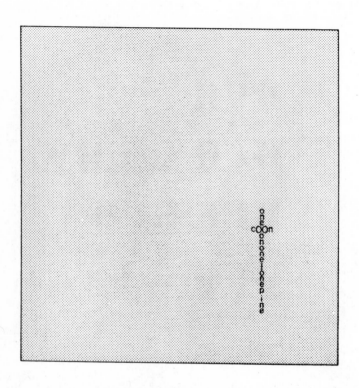

RED-BONE HEAVEN

THOMAS A. CLARK

One tablespoonful of this mixture
to be taken three times a day

Thyme & Tide

SHAKE THE BOTTLE BEFORE TAKING EACH DOSE.

EMMETT WILLIAMS

she loves me

she loves me not

she loves

she loves me

she

she loves

she

like   attracts   like
like   attracts   like
like   attracts   like
like   attracts   like
like   attracts   like
like   attracts   like
like   attracts   like
likeattractslike
likeattractlike
likattraclike
likttradike
likteralike
liktelikts

JANE AUGUSTINE
Variations on UI

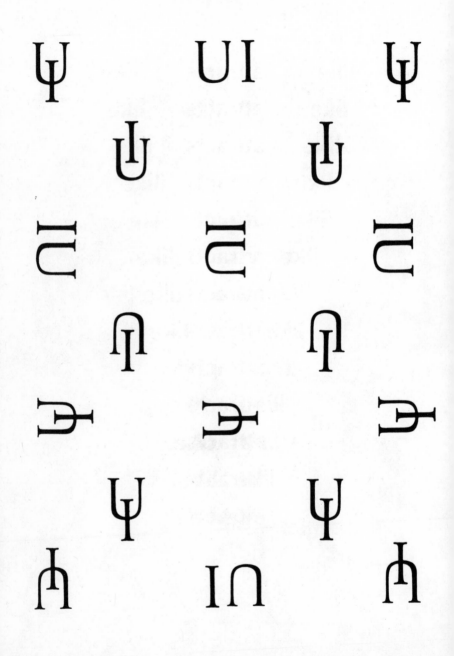

Core

RONALD JOHNSON
from *The Songs of the Earth*

W A N E

W a n e w
  a A n e N w
    a A n e N w E

W a n e w
  a A n e N w
    a A n e N w E

W A N E

A N E W
A N E W
A N E W
A N E W

KATHY SCHENKEL

over and   over and
over and   over and
over and   over and
over and   over and
over and   over and
over and   over and
over and   over and
over and   over and
over and   over and
over and   over and
over and   over and
over and   over and
over and   over and
over and   over and
over and   over and
over and   over and
over and   over and
over and   over again

      over and   over and
over and   over and

      over and   over and
over and   over and

      over and   over and
over and   over and

      over and   over and
over and   over and

      over and   over and
over and   over and

      over and   over end

RICHARD KOSTELANETZ

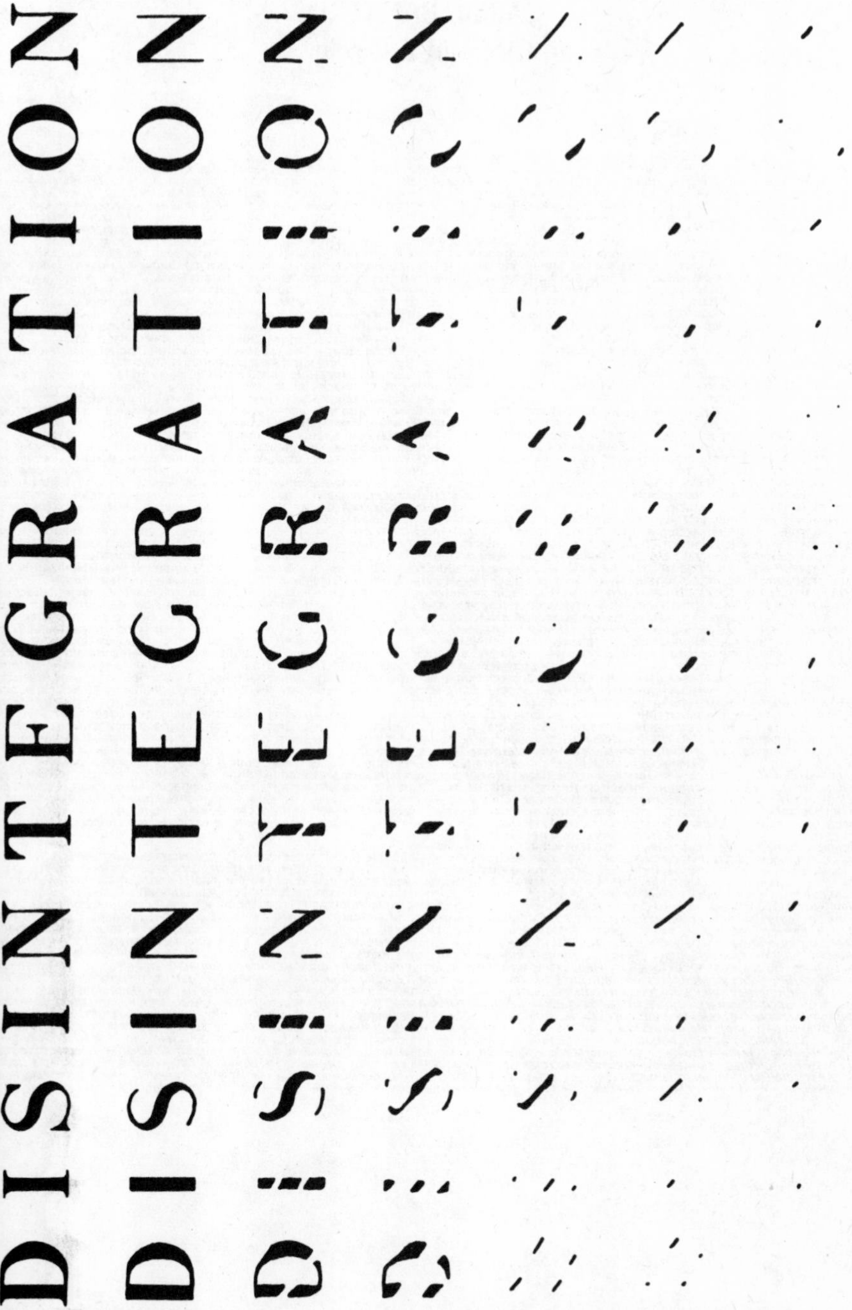
DISINTEGRATION
DISINTEGRATION

CAROL BANKERD
Circle in a Circle

(A visual text work composed of the continuously repeated phrase "circleinacircleinacircle…" arranged in dense horizontal lines to form a rectangular field.)

Me-We

```
MEMEMEMEMEMEMEMEMEMEME
MEMEMEMEMEMEMEMEMEMEME
MEMEMEMEMEMEMEMEMEMEME
MEMEMEMEMEMEMEMEMEMEME
MEMEMEMEMEMEMEMEMEMEME
MEMEMEMEMEMEMEMEMEMEME
MEMEMEMEMEMEMEMEMEMEME
MEMEMEMEMEMEMEMEMEMEME
MEMEMEMEMEMEMEMEMEMEME
MEMEMEMEMEMEMEMEMEMEME
MEMEMEMEMEMEMEMEMEMEME
MEMEMEMEMEMEMEMEMEMEME
MEMEMEMEMEMEMEMEMEMEME
MEMEMEMEMEMEMEMEMEMEME
MEMEMEMEMEMEMEMEMEMEME
MEMEMEMEMEMEMEMEMEMEME
WEWEWEWEWEWEWEWEWEWEWE
WEWEWEWEWEWEWEWEWEWEWE
WEWEWEWEWEWEWEWEWEWEWE
WEWEWEWEWEWEWEWEWEWEWE
WEWEWEWEWEWEWEWEWEWEWE
WEWEWEWEWEWEWEWEWEWEWE
WEWEWEWEWEWEWEWEWEWEWE
WEWEWEWEWEWEWEWEWEWEWE
WEWEWEWEWEWEWEWEWEWEWE
WEWEWEWEWEWEWEWEWEWEWE
WEWEWEWEWEWEWEWEWEWEWE
WEWEWEWEWEWEWEWEWEWEWE
WEWEWEWEWEWEWEWEWEWEWE
```

JOHN FURNIVAL
Semiotic Folk Poem

Lexical Key

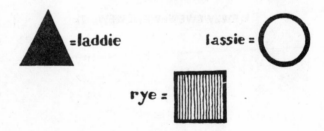

Devil Trap

Rocket I

Rocket II

FERDINAND KRIWET
Dreamerican

Lesebogen VI

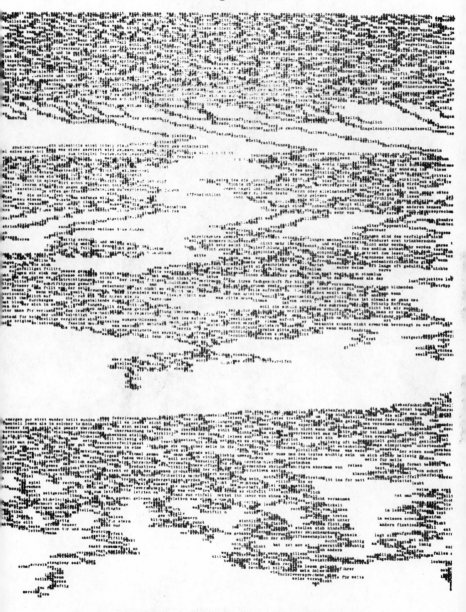

This might have been the view, stretching as far out as the eye can read, seen from the top of the Tower of Babel.

JORDAN STECKEL
Logopolis

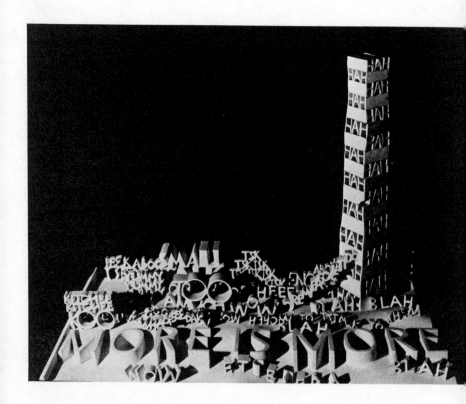

This is a district of a vast logopolis, still under construction by sculptor Jordan Steckel, from the same realm as Kriwet's **Lesebogen.**

RUBE GOLDBERG
Self-Emptying Ashtray of the Future

Bright Romantic moon brings love birds (A) together on perch (B), causing string (C) to upset sprinkling can (D) and wet shirt (E). Shirt shrinks, unveiling portrait (F). Dog (G), seeing portrait of his master, wags tail, brushing ashes from tray into asbestos bag (H). Smouldering butts ignite rocket (I) which carries bag of ashes out the window into the far reaches of the sky.

Reuben Lucius Goldberg's cartoon-blueprints of inventions were always far-out, but sometimes also as practical as Leonardo da Vinci's. In this case (patent applied for in the 1930s), he seems to have anticipated a method for disposing of radioactive wastes currently under solemn consideration by the Atomic Energy Commission.

KATHLEEN FERGUSON
A Toothsome Romance

1.
Yes, it was the Tooth Prom at the "Stars Fell on Miami Ballroom" in the heart of the great American mouthland.

2.
The teeth danced to and fro.

3.
The music played and the stars fell like crazy.

4.
Then she saw "him"— standing in the corner looking over all the local enamel.

5.
For a brief moment the world still stood. Their eyes met—*zap!*

6.
They danced the night away—well, until he got a nifty idea. He asked, "Why don't you come to my apartment and look at my collection of floss?"

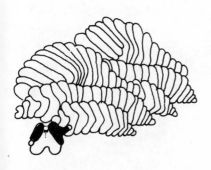

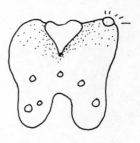

7.
When they arrived he casually pointed to a heap of old crescent rolls, claiming that he kept them there out of charity. All, he said, suffered from some form of incipient botulism, creeping crud, or tertiary ptomaine.

8.
Suddenly the clock struck midnight. He began to change. Dark spots appeared. . . .

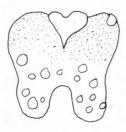

9.
Then more dark spots and stains appeared. What pain! "Out, out, damned spots!" he shouted, but they wouldn't go. At last he said, "Molly, I guess I'd better tell you the whole story. . . ."

10.
"I used to eat a balanced diet of carrots & cabbage . . ."

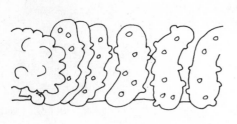

11.
". . . and cucumbers . . ."

12.
". . . with milk from my own special white-and-brown fur bottle."

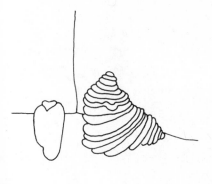

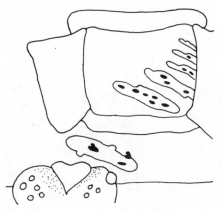

13.
"Then I met Caramel Crescent. I became very attached to her—she being the little sugar-coated cutie she was."

14.
"One day some chocolate-chip cookies floated in through the window."

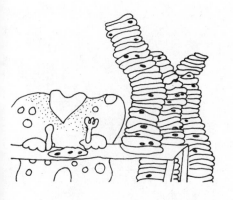

15.
"I ate them for breakfast, lunch, and dinner, and for snacks in between."

16.
"The chips in the chocolate-chip cookies grew in size. Oh, how I loved them! Lick, lick, lick. . . ."

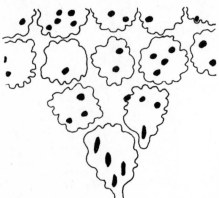

17.
"Lick, climb, lick, lick, climb, climb. . . ."

18.
"How luscious they were! But I needed a faster way to snorf them up."

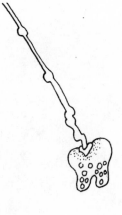

19.
"I was getting worn down to a stump. So . . ."

20.
"I began to mainline them. That is why, Molly, I'm now an Appaloosa of dental decay. I'm *hooked*."

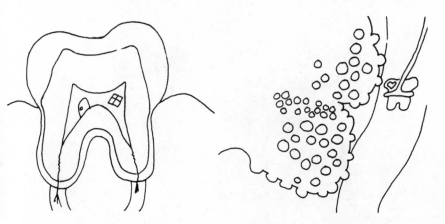

21.
She froze there, numb, then peered deeply into her innermost self, X-ray style.

22.
She knew that he would infect any tooth he came close to, that he deserved a severe tongue-lashing, at least to be drilled and filled, maybe even yanked out, but . . .

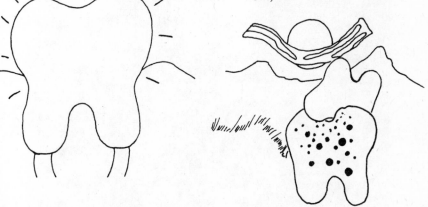

23.
. . . but something about him appealed to her. "Harry," she told him, "I still care—and if you care for me the way I care for you, we'll find a cure for our caries together."

24.
And so, cusped together, smiling bravely, they turned toward the sunnyside-up (with cloud strip) of a bright new day.

ZaZu

This mysterious ZaZu, who might be Isis or Astarte or Aphrodite or any of the other theomorphoses of the great goddess, has here descended to Earth and even become involved in the democratic process. As seems clearly evident in the above graffiti inscribed on the door (locked from the inside) of the Girls room of a high school somewhere in the inner city.

On which high hermetic note, we conclude. . . .

Biographical Notes and Index

APOLLINAIRE, GUILLAUME (1880–1918), born in Rome, the illegitimate son of a Bourbon army officer, Francesco Flugi d'Aspermont, and a Polish noblewoman, Olga de Kostrowitzky. Apollinaire was educated and spent most of his creative life in France, where he died of wounds suffered while fighting at the front during World War I just as the Armistice was signed. He was the friend and critical champion of the painters Braque, Picasso, Matisse, Dufy, Derain and others of the School of Paris during their formative years. Apollinaire once described his poetics as "an idealization of free verse and of typographical precision at a time when typography is brilliantly ending its career, at the dawn of new methods of reproduction, the cinema and the gramophone. . . ." Works include: *Le Bestiaire* (1911); *Alcools* (1913); *Calligrammes* (1918). **p. 192**

ARP, (Hans) JEAN (1887–   ), born in Strasbourg, France. Arp changed his first name from Hans to Jean when his native Alsace was returned to France following the Armistice ending World War I. A cofounder, along with Tristan Tzara, of the Dadaist movement, he is best known for his sculpture, but his work in other media and his critical theories were equally influential. **p. 200**

AUGUSTINE, JANE. The poet was educated at Bryn Mawr and at Washington University in St. Louis, and teaches at present at John Jay College, CUNY. She has contributed to various "little" magazines as well as to feminist anthologies. **p. 296**

AYRES, PHILIP (1638–1712), born in London. Ayres's chief work, *Lyric Poems,* published in 1687, consists mainly of translations and imitations of Italian and Spanish poets popular at the time. He was a lifelong friend and associate of John Dryden. **p. 100**

AZEREDO, RONALDO (1937–   ), born in Rio de Janeiro. The poet has contributed to the Brazilian review *Invençao,* and his work has been republished in anthologies of Concrete poetry in the United States and abroad. **p. 261**

BALL, HUGO (1886–1927), born in Germany. Ball, a poet and critic, was one of the most active proponents of Dadaism in Europe following World War I. **p. 198**

BANKERD, CAROL (1941–   ), born in Grosse Pointe, Michigan. Ms. Bankerd was educated at Yale University, where she received an M.S.A. degree. She taught for several years at Princeton, and at present teaches visual studies at Hunter College. Her *Graphic Poems* appeared in 1969. **p. 304**

BLAKE, WILLIAM (1757–1827), born in London. The son of a small tradesman in hosiery, Blake received little formal schooling, and was taught to read and write by his mother. At the age of ten he entered a school to learn drawing, and subsequently was apprenticed to the engraver Basire. With the aid of his wife, Blake engraved and then colored his illuminated books of poems by a unique process that, he claimed, had been revealed to him in a vision by his deceased brother Robert. **p. 122**

BREMER, CLAUS (1924–   ), born in Hamburg, Germany. Bremer, an early exponent of Concrete poetry, has also done significant work in experimental theater and in publishing. Books include: *poésie* (1954); *ideogramme* (1964). **p. 282**

BROWN, BOB (1886–1959). Brown was one of the liveliest members of the American expatriate colony in France during the years between World Wars I and II. In the preface to his book of picture-poetry, *1450–1950,* published by the Black Sun Press in Paris in 1929, he wrote: "I try to express myself in optical poems, as Apollinaire and Cummings try. . . . I think we need to recapture something of the healthy hieroglyphic, now that oratory is dead." **p. 208**

BUNYAN, JOHN (1628–1688), born in Bedfordshire, England. The self-educated son of an artisan, Bunyan served during the Civil War with the rebel forces, after which he became a preacher and the leader of a Baptist sect. As the unwobbling pivot of the Puritan conscience, he refused to submit following the restoration of Charles II, and spent twelve years in prison. It was while he was in captivity that he wrote his great *The Pilgrim's Progress from this World to That which is to Come,* published in two parts, the first in 1674 and the second in 1684. Among his other works are: *Grace Abounding* (1666); *The Life and Death of Mr. Badman* (1680); and *The Holy War* (1682). **p. 106**

BURKE, KENNETH (1897–   ), born in Pittsburgh, Pa. Though best known as a literary and social critic, Burke has also exploded into symbolic action as a poet at various times throughout his career. Of his "Flowerishes," he writes that they are variants of the "momentarily summarizing." Works include: *Collected Poems 1915–1967*. **p. 206**

CALVERT, EDWARD (1799–1883), born in Devonshire, Kent. Calvert served as a midshipman in the Royal Navy during his youth and spent several years voyaging throughout the Mediterranean. He was profoundly influenced by Blake's poetry and pictures, and taught himself how to engrave on wood and copper. Even when Calvert was in his eighties, he would make an annual pilgrimage to the house in London where he had first met Blake. **p. 142**

CAMPION, THOMAS (1567–1637), born in London. A physician as well as a poet, Campion began his literary career as a disciple of Sir

Philip Sidney, with whose *Astrophel and Stella,* published in 1591, his early lyrics first appeared. He wrote both songs and music for several masques produced at court. In his famous critical work, *Observations in the Art of English Poesie,* Campion sought to extend the range of English verse by attuning accentual and quantitative meters. **p. 68**

CARROLL, LEWIS (1832–1898), born at Datesbury, near Cheshire. Carroll (whose real name was Charles Lutwidge Dodgson) taught mathematics and logic for many years at Christ Church, Oxford. In appearance he is said to have been thin, of moderate height, with a handsome but slightly askew face—the level of his eyes was not the same—and to have walked stiffly braced and jerkily. Carroll was a deacon in the Church of England, but seldom preached because of a stammer. Though he loved little girls, he loathed little boys. **p. 154**

CATS, JACOB (1577–1660), born in Brouwershaven, Holland, "Father" Cats, as he was affectionately known, was a statesman and diplomat as well as a poet. He headed embassies to England in 1627 and again in 1651–52, and rose to high political office in the United Netherlands. Works include: *Emblemata* (1618); and *De Spiegel van den ouden and nieuwen Tijdt* ("The Mirror of Old and New Times") (1632). **p. 110**

CLARE, JOHN (1793–1864), born in Helpston, Northamptonshire. Brought up in poverty as the son of a field laborer supported by parish relief, Clare began to compose his visionary poems almost as soon as he learned how to write. After his *Poems Descriptive of Rural Life and Scenery,* "by a Northamptonshire peasant," appeared in 1820, he was patronized and extolled as a new Burns by the literati of London, but their attention waned in later years. Clare, old and forgotten, ended his life in an asylum for the mentally ill. **p. 137**

CLARK, THOMAS A. (1944–   ), born in Greenock, Scotland. Clark's poems and "inventions" have earned him an underground reputation in literary catacombs in England and the United States. He is a founding member of "Experiment in Disintegrating Language." Works include: *North Bohemian Coalfields* (1970); *Some Particulars* (1971). **p. 293**

CRASHAW, RICHARD (1612–1649), born in London. Though reared in a devout Protestant household by a clergyman father, Crashaw became a convert to the Catholic faith and sought refuge on the continent. He died at the age of thirty-seven in Loreto, Italy, where he had a minor post in the Church hierarchy. His *Carmen Deo Nostro* was published posthumously in Paris in 1652. **p. 70**

CUMMINGS, E. E. (1894–1962), born in Cambridge, Massachusetts. Cummings was equally dedicated throughout his career to painting and to poetry. He is the author of a classical book of memoirs on his experiences in a prison camp in France during World War I (*The Enormous Room*, 1922); plays in prose and verse (*Him*, 1926); a travel book on Russia (*Eimi*, 1933), as well as fairy tales, art criticism, reviews, etc. For four decades he lived and worked in Patchin Place in Greenwich Village. **p. 203**

CUTTS, SIMON (1944–   ), born in Derby, England. He has been coeditor with Stuart Mills of Tarasque Press since 1964 in Nottingham. Cutts has published many pamphlets and articles. He is currently engaged in publishing a list of collaborative ventures with many visual artists, as well as making and distributing constructed poems and objects. Works include: *Claude Monet in His Water Garden* (1967); *Camouflage, Gallery Number 10* (1968); *A New Kind of Tie: Poems 1966–68* (1972). **p. 232**

DE CAMPOS, AUGUSTO (1931–   ), born in São Paulo, Brazil. De Campos, along with his brother Haraldo and various other co-spirits in São Paulo during the early '50s, founded the "Noigandres" movement for Concrete poetry. He describes his work as a "tension of things-words in space-time." **p. 260**

DE NIRO, ROBERT (1922–   ), born in Syracuse, New York. De Niro (not to be confused with the actor of the same name, his son) is one of the leading members of the New York School of painters. His work has been exhibited in galleries and museums throughout the United States and abroad. **p. 169**

DE VREE, PAUL (1909–   ), born in Antwerp, Belgium. One of the earliest Concrete poets in Europe, de Vree is also well known as a novelist and filmmaker. Works include: *Egelronde* (1957); *Throw In* (1959); *explositieven* (1966). **p. 253**

DÖHL, REINHARD (1934–   ), born in Wallenschied, Germany. Döhl, whose Concrete poems have been widely reprinted in anthologies, now makes his home in Stuttgart. Works include: *prosa zum beispiel* (1965); *4 texte* (1965); *es anna* (1966). **p. 281**

DONNE, JOHN (1571–1631), born in London. According to Ben Jonson, Donne wrote "all of his best pieces ere he was twenty-five years old"—that is, during the 1590s—but they were not collected and published until 1633, two years after his death. In the same year, incidentally, George Herbert's *The Temple* first appeared. **p. 49**

EDSON, RUSSELL (1928–   ), born in New York City. Russell's haunted prose-poems, and the cryptic drawings that accompany them, have their roots indubitably in Dada, but also in American comic strips. Works include: *The Very Thing That Happens* (1964); *The Clam Theatre* (1973). **p. 220**

FARLEY, ROBERT(*fl.* 1638), born in Scotland. Farley, or Farlie, or "Roberto Farlaeo, Scoto-Britanno," as he sometimes plumed himself, published his *Lychnocausia, Lights Moral Emblems* in 1638. **p. 96**

FERGUSON, KATHLEEN (1945–), born in Chicago, Illinois. A sculptor as well as a graphic artist, Ms. Ferguson studied at the Rhode Island School of Design, and has taught at several universities in the United States. She has exhibited her sculpture widely in galleries and museums, including a one-woman show at the Smithsonian. **p. 314**

FINLAY, IAN HAMILTON (1925–), born in Scotland. Finlay is perhaps the chief exponent of Concrete poetry in England and the United States. He is founder of the Wild Hawthorn Press in Scotland. Works include: *The Dancers Inherit the Party* (1959); *Telegrams from My Windmill* (1964); *Poems to Hear and See* (1971). **p. 245**

FORD, CHARLES HENRI (1910–), born in the United States. Ford was for many years the editor of the surrealist magazine *View*, which served as a two-way mirror for American and European poets and painters during the '40s and '50s. *Spare Parts,* from which the items in this *Gallery* were taken, was published in Athens in 1966. Works include: *The Overturned Lake* (1941); *Sleep in a Nest of Flames* (1949). **p. 210**

FURNIVAL, JOHN (1933–), born in London. Furnival studied at the Royal College of Art in London, and has exhibited widely in England and abroad. He is coeditor of the Openings Press. **p. 306**

GERZ, JOCHEN (1940–), born in Berlin. Gerz lives at present in Paris, where he is coeditor of the Agentzia Press. His work has appeared in several anthologies of Concrete poetry. **p. 280**

GOLDBERG, REUBEN LUCIUS (1883–1970), born in San Francisco. "Rube" Goldberg, whose cartoon inventions appeared in American newspapers for more than half a century, has lately been beatified as a sort of Luddite saint of the ecology movement in the United States. **p. 313**

GOMRINGER, EUGEN (1924–), born in Bolivia. Gomringer is not only one of the founding fathers of Concrete poetry, but also its best-known European practitioner. He makes his home in Switzerland, and, through the Eugen Gomringer Press, publishes the work of several of the leading poets in the movement. Books include: *Die Konstellationem* (1964); *Manifeste und Darstellungen der Konkreten Poesie* (1966). **p. 239**

HARVEY, CHRISTOPHER (1597–1663), born in London. Harvey's volume of devotional poetry, *The Synagogue* (1640), written in imitation of George Herbert, was often bound up in one book with Herbert's *The Temple.* **p. 90**

HERBERT, GEORGE (1593–1633), born in Wales. The younger brother of the poet Lord Herbert of Cherbury, Herbert was reared by his gifted mother, who was a friend of John Donne. He served as Public Orator from 1620–27 at Trinity College, Cambridge, and in 1626 was ordained a deacon, and in 1630 a priest, in the Church of England. His poems in English circulated only in manuscript during his lifetime. Shortly before his death, he sent them to his friend Nicholas Ferrar, founder of the religious community of Little Gidding, with the request that he decide whether to publish or to burn them all. Under the title *The Temple,* they first appeared in 1633. **p. 50**

HERRICK, ROBERT (1591–1674), born in London. The most illustrious of the poetic "sons of Ben" (Jonson), Herrick spent ten years as an apprentice goldsmith in his family's firm in London. He left to study at Cambridge University, where he took an M.A. in 1620. In later years he served as a vicar of Dean Prior in Exeter. The poem published in this book is the end piece of his *Hesperides* (1648). **p. 52**

HIGGINS, DICK (1938–   ), born in Cambridge, England. Higgins has also composed music, produced films, and written criticism on a variety of subjects. He is the founder of the Something Else Press. Works include: *A Book About Love & Death* (1972). **p. 231**

HOLLANDER, JOHN (1929–   ), born in New York City. Hollander's figured poems are said to "contemplate the objects or forms whose silhouettes shape their very lines on the page." Works include: *The Untuning of the Sky: Ideas of Music in English Poetry, 1500–1700* (1961); *Movie Going and Other Poems* (1962); *Visions from the Ramble* (1965); *Types of Shape* (1969). **p. 226**

JOYCE, JAMES (1882–1941), born in Dublin. Joyce's towering babble of a book, *Finnegans Wake,* has been acclaimed by critics as the most prodigious erection of the Word in our time. Once, when asked what it was all about, the author Samuel Beckett, a close friend and associate of Joyce, replied: "It is not about something. It *is* that something itself." **p. 201**

JOHNSON, RONALD (1935–   ), born in Ashland, Kansas. Concerning his sequence *Songs of the Earth* (designed and printed by Grabhorn-Hoyem in 1970), Johnson writes: "These translations and responses might properly be called 'strains'–as in a strain of music or poetry, but also those words and notes which strain their limits outward toward the unutterable." Works include: *The Book of the Green Man* (1969). **p. 298**

JONSON, BEN (1572–1637), born in London. The son of a clergyman who died in the year of his birth, Jonson was raised by his mother, who later married a master bricklayer of Westminster. His early youth was spent as an apprentice bricklayer, as a soldier serving in Flanders, and, following his marriage in 1594, as an actor. His first extant play, *Every Man in His Humour,* in which Shakespeare appeared as an actor, was produced in 1598, and established him as one of the leading playwrights in London. Jonson wrote more than twenty-five masques for the court of James I, collaborating with the architect and stage designer Inigo Jones. **p. 64**

KAMIIE, FUMIO (1947–   ), born in Hokkaido, Japan. After graduating from the Tama Art-University, where he studied the fine arts, he became a painter. He now lives in Tokyo. **p. 276**

KAMIMURA, HIRO (1930–   ), born in Tokyo. Kamimura, in addition to his own Concrete poetry, is highly regarded for his translations of German literature into Japanese. He currently teaches poetry at the University of Osaka. **p. 279**

KOSTELANETZ, RICHARD (1940–   ), born in New York City. Kostelanetz prefers to call his works "word-imagery," in order to encompass (as he writes) "the two major genres of the form—imaged words and worded images. The distinction depends upon whether word or image is the base." He is a widely known critic and anthologist as well as a poet. Works include: *Imaged Word & Worded Image* (1970); *Visual Language* (1970); *Possibilities of Poetry* (1970); *The End of Intelligent Writing* (1974). **p. 301**

KRIWET, FERDINAND (1942–   ), born in Dusseldorf, Germany. Kriwet, besides his picture-poems, has produced movies, collages, "happenings," etc. His works have been widely anthologized both in Europe and in the United States. Works include: *Leserattenfaenge* (1965); *Apollo Amerika* (1969). **p. 310**

LEAR, EDWARD (1812–1888), born in London. The youngest of twenty-one children of a Danish father and Irish mother, he himself remained unmarried, but lived happily for seventeen years with a cat named Foss, whom he never tired of sketching. Lear was an expert photographer, musician, and painter of watercolors, and served as a teacher of drawing to Queen Victoria. Though he seldom drank, he had a blasted proboscis, like that of J. P. Morgan or W. C. Fields, about which he wrote his famous threnody, "The Dong with a Luminous Nose." His *Nonsense* was first published in London in 1871. **p. 146**

LINDSAY, VACHEL (1879–1931), born in Springfield, Illinois. Lindsay must have learned how to conduct his own callithumpian brass band, heard in such works as "The Congo" and "General William Booth Enters Heaven," from Edgar Allan Poe, to whom he pays tribute in the selection in this book. A skillful artist, he illustrated his own works and designed a number of picture-poems. **p. 168**

MALLARMÉ, STÉPHANE (1842–1898), born in Paris. Mallarmé at the age of twenty went to England in order to learn, he said, enough of the language to read Edgar Allan Poe in the original. After remaining there for nine months, he returned to his native land doomed to teach English in *lycées* for the next thirty years. Though his life seemed outwardly humdrum and uneventful, Mallarmé became the most revolutionary poet of his age, the acknowledged master of the Symbolist movement in France. **p. 170**

MARINETTI, EMILIO FILIPPO TOMMASO (1876–1944), born in Italy. Marinetti was the founder and chief theoretician of the Italian Futurist movement in art and poetry. Much of the rhetoric of Futurism, as well as many of its doctrines, were later incorporated by Mussolini into Fascist ideology. **p. 199**

MAYER, HANSJÖRG (1943–), born in Stuttgart, Germany. Mayer has been acclaimed as "poetypographer" for his designs and innovations. He writes of his alphabet: "They do not relate to other letters with which they might form a word, but exclusively to their own visual shape. . . ." Works include: *typoactions* (1967). **p. 283**

MENEZES, FLORIVALDO (1931–), born in Brazil. Menezes, whose work has been reproduced in magazines and anthologies throughout the world, is associated with the "Noigandres" movement in São Paulo. **p. 264**

MERTON, THOMAS (1915–1968), born in France. After a restless search for spiritual fulfillment in modern art and radical politics, Merton became a convert to Catholicism and entered a Trappist monastery in 1938. The story of his conversion is related in *The Seven Story Mountain*, published in 1941. About a year before his accidental death in Bangkok, while on a pilgrimage to Asia, he became increasingly involved with Concrete poetry. The poem in this book first appeared in 1968 in *Monk's Pond*, a magazine Merton edited from the Abbey of Gethsemani in the United States. **p. 230**

MIDDLETON, CHRISTOPHER (1923–), born in Cornwall, England. Middleton has written libretti for opera and has also translated German and Italian poetry into English. "Homage to Kafka," included in this book, is one of several poems he has composed in the genre. Works include: *Nonsequences* (1965); *Our Flowers & Nice Bones* (1969). **p. 228**

MORGAN, EDWIN (1920–), born in Glasgow. The poet currently teaches English literature at the University of Glasgow. Works include: *Starryveldt* (1965); *The Second Life* (1968); *The Horseman's Word* (1970). **p. 229**

NIIKUNI, SEIICHI (1925–   ), born in Japan. Niikuni is the most innovative and best known of the Concrete poets in Japan. Works include: *Zero On* (1963); *Poèmes franco-japonais* (with Pierre Garnier) (1966). **p. 271**

OCKERSE, TOM (1940–   ), born in Holland. Ockerse, educated in the United States, currently teaches at the University of Indiana. His picture-poems have been widely exhibited in galleries and reprinted in anthologies both here and abroad. Works include: *The A-Z Book* (1969). **p. 284**

PALMER, SAMUEL (1805–1881), born in Walworth, near London. When Palmer first saw the woodcuts Blake had made to illustrate Vergil's *Eclogues,* he referred to them ecstatically as "corners of Paradise; models of the exquisitest pitch of intense poetry." Under the influence of Blake, Palmer painted his own enchanted landscapes of the country around Shoreham during his youth. In his later years, however, the visionary gleam fled and faded from his pictures. **p. 140**

PATCHEN, KENNETH (1911–1972), born in Ohio. Patchen suffered from a spinal illness throughout his life. Nonetheless, he produced numerous books of poems, picture-poems, novels, fairy tales, criticism, and etceterogeneous works. He lived for many years in New York's Greenwich Village. Works include: *Because It Is* (1960); *But Even So* (1968); *Collected Poems* (1968). **p. 212**

PEACHAM, HENRY (?1578–1642?), born at North Mimms, Hertfordshire. Peacham attended Trinity College, Cambridge, where he was awarded the M.A. degree in 1598; and he also studied painting and engraving in the Netherlands. His *The Art of Drawing with the Pen and Limning in Water Colors* (1606), was the first book of practical instruction of that kind to appear in England. For his Emblem book, *Minerva Britanna, or A Garden of Heroical Devises* (1612), Peacham drew heavily upon Ripa's *Iconologia* and also upon Spenser's *The Fairie Queene.* He is perhaps best known for his "courtesy" book, *The Compleat Gentleman* (1622). **p. 60**

POUND, EZRA (1885–1972), born in Hailey, Idaho. Pound up to the end of his life was the most controversial as well as influential poet of the twentieth century. The rare item in this book, done in collaboration with the anthropologist Jaime de Angulo, is from a volume of miscellanies, *Pavannes and Divigations,* published in 1958. **p. 202**

PUTTENHAM, GEORGE (c. 1529–1590). Little is known of Puttenham's early life and literary career, but his *The Arte of English Poesie,* published anonymously a year before his death, remains as one of the chief critical documents of the Elizabethan age. At one time the book was wrongly attributed to his brother Richard. **p. 46**

QUARLES, FRANCIS (1592–1644), born in Essex, England. The son of a surveyor-general for the navy, Quarles was educated at Cambridge. From 1626 to 1630, he served in Ireland as secretary to Archbishop Ussher; and in 1640, he was appointed chronologer to the city of London. Though he was the most highly esteemed poet of his age, upon his death, Quarles left his widow in poverty with nine of their eighteen children. His first book, *A Feast for Worms,* published in 1620, sounded the groan of pious misery that was to remain the keynote of 17th century religious poetry. **p. 72**

RIPA, CESARE (c.1560–c.1623), born in Perugia, Italy. Ripa, whose real name was Giovanni Campani, modeled his immensely popular and influential *Iconologia* upon the works of Horapollo and Alciati. First published without illustrations in 1593, it went through numerous editions, during which new allegorical figures were added by various artists. The last edition was published in Mexico as late as 1886. **p. 102**

SCHENKEL, KATHY. The poet was born in Fort Wayne, Indiana and received her education at the University of Illinois. Her work has appeared in several anthologies of Concrete poetry, as well as the magazine *Subvers.* **p. 299**

SMART, CHRISTOPHER (1722–1771), born in Shipbourne, Kent, England. Smart was educated at Pembroke Hall, Cambridge, where his early poems and translations received the praise of Pope. He became a member of the literary circle of Samuel Johnson, which included Garrick, Boswell, Fielding, Burney, and other worthies. His *Jubilate Agno (Rejoice in the Lamb),* from which the poems in this book are taken, was composed by him while he was confined in a madhouse. The manuscript, long considered lost, was rediscovered and published in 1939. **p. 120**

SMITH, STEVIE (Florence Margaret Smith) (1902–1970), born in Yorkshire, England. Stevie Smith not only "illuminated" her own poems but also set them to music and sang them as well at arts festivals in England. Works include: *Selected Poems* (1964). **p. 216**

SOLT, MARY ELLEN (1920–   ), born in Gilmore City, Iowa. The author was turned on to Concrete poetry, and inspired to produce her celebrated *Flowers in Concrete* (1966), in collaboration with the typographer John Dearstyne, after a visit to Ian Hamilton Finlay's studio in Scotland. Her anthology *Concrete Poetry: A World View*

(1969) contains a valuable critical introduction to the movement. She currently teaches at the University of Indiana. Works include: *The Peoplemover: A Demonstration Poem* (1969). **p. 256**

STECKEL, JORDAN (1930–   ), born in New York City. Steckel's "crowd faces," Daumier-like sculptured caricatures of the multifaceted face of humanity, have been exhibited throughout the U.S. He maintains his studio in New York City, where he is completing his "Logopolis" after ten years of alternate construction and demolition. **p. 312**

STEVENSON, ROBERT LOUIS (1850–1894), born in Edinburgh, Scotland. The son of an engineer, Stevenson was educated at the University of Edinburgh, and began his literary career as an essayist and author of travel impressions of France. During a visit to California in 1879, he married an American widow, Mrs. Osbourne, for whose son he did the Emblem poems reproduced in this book. Toward the end of his life, suffering from tuberculosis, he set out on a long sea voyage to the South Pacific and settled on the island of Samoa in 1891. **p. 164**

SUNADA, CHIMA (1944–   ), born in Kofu, in central Japan. After graduating from the Tokyo Kyoiku-University, where she studied calligraphy, Ms. Sunada became a teacher of the art in Tokyo. **p. 277**

SWENSON, MAY (1919–   ), born in Logan, Utah. In her *Iconographs* (1970), from which the poems in this book were taken, Ms. Swenson describes her intention as follows: "To cause an instant object-to-eye encounter with each poem before it is read word-after-word; to have simultaneity as well as sequence." Works include: *To Mix with Time* (1963); *Half Sun, Half Sleep* (1967). **p. 224**

TAVARES, SALETTE. Ms. Tavares' poems have appeared in the magazine *Ivençao*. Her work has been anthologized in several volumes of Concrete poetry. **p. 259**

TURNER, JOSEPH MALLORD WILLIAM (1775–1851), born in London. The son of a barber and wig-maker, Turner received little formal education and, even as an artist, was largely self-taught. Throughout his career he composed poems as reflections upon, and extensions of, his paintings. The most ambitious of these literary works was a philosophical narrative, *The Fallacies of Hope*, which he began around 1812. It was never completed. **p. 144**

WHITNEY, GEOFFREY (c. 1548–1601), born at Coole Pilate, near Nantwich, Chesire. Whitney was educated at Magdalene College, Cambridge, where his literary gifts won him the patronage of the Earl of Leicester. In 1586 he moved to Leyden, Holland, and enrolled at the University of Leyden. That same year his *A Choice of Emblemes and*

Other Devises was printed by François Raphelengien, at the printing house of Christophe Plantin in Leyden, and quickly became one of the most successful as well as influential books of its kind in England. **p. 28**

WILLIAMS, EMMETT (1925–   ), born in Greenville, South Carolina. The poet describes the visual element in his work as ". . . structural, a consequence of the poem, a 'picture' of the lines of force of the work itself, and not merely textural." His *An Anthology of Concrete Poetry* (1967) offers a wide view of the movement. Works include: *An Anecdoted Topography of Chance* (1966); *sweethearts* (1967). **p. 294**

WILLIAMS, JONATHAN (1929–   ), born in Ashville, North Carolina. As founder and editor of the Jargon Press, Williams has published the work of Charles Olson, Robert Creeley, Louis Zukovsky, Mina Loy, and many younger poets. His own poems have been widely anthologized. Works include: *An Ear in Bartram's Tree* (1969); *Blues & Roots/Rue & Bluets* (1971). **p. 288**

WITHER, GEORGE (1588–1667), born in Hampshire, England. Called "wretched Wither" by Alexander Pope both for his crabbed meters and his zealous religiosity, Wither was deeply engaged in the revolutionary politics of his age. He was imprisoned several times, the first in 1613 for a satire on the monarchy called *Abuses Stript and Whipt,* and the last in 1660, when he was seventy-two years old, for an unpublished poem against the Restoration of Charles II. **p. 80**

XISTO, PEDRO (1901–   ), born in Pernambuco, Brazil. The poet has served as cultural attaché for Brazil in Tokyo. **p. 262**

YOSHIZAWA, SHOJI (1937–   ), born in Shizuoka, eastern Japan. After graduating from the Musashing Art-University, where he studied commercial art, he is now a graphic artist and lives in Tokyo. **p. 275**

ZAZU is ZaZu. The photograph is from the collection of Robert Reisner. **p. 302**

Selected Bibliography

Boas, George. *The Hieroglyphics of Horapollo*. New Jersey: Bollingen Series 23, Princeton University Press, 1950.

Cohn, Robert. *Mallarmé's Masterwork*. Paris: Mouton & Co., 1966.

Freeman, Rosemary. *English Emblem Books*. London: Chatto & Windus, 1948.

Gardner, Martin. *The Annotated Alice*. New York: Bramhall House, 1970.

Hagstrum, Jean. *William Blake: Poet and Painter*. Chicago: University of Chicago Press, 1964.

Lee, Rensselaer. *Ut Pictura Poesis: The Humanistic Theory of Painting*. New York: W. W. Norton & Co., 1967.

Liu, James. *The Art of Chinese Poetry*. Chicago: University of Chicago Press, 1962.

Panofsky, Erwin. *Idea: A Concept in Art Theory*. New York: Harper & Row, 1968.

Praz, Mario. *Studies in Seventeenth Century Imagery*. Rome: Edizioni di Storia e Letteratura, 1964.

Raine, Kathleen. *Blake and Tradition*. New Jersey: Bollingen Series XXXV-11, Princeton University Press, 1968.

Reisner, Robert. *Graffiti*. New York: Cowles Book Co., 1971.

Solt, Mary Ellen, with Willis Barnstone, co-editor. *Concrete Poetry: A World View*. Bloomington: Indiana University Press, 1969.

Warren, Austin. *Richard Crashaw: A Study in Baroque Sensibility*. Ann Arbor: University of Michigan Press, 1957.

Williams, Emmett. *An Anthology of Concrete Poetry*. New York: Something Else Press, 1967.

Wind, Edgar. *Pagan Mysteries in the Renaissance*. New York: W. W. Norton & Co., 1968.

Yates, Francis. *Giordano Bruno and the Hermetic Tradition*. New York: Vintage Books, 1969.